W. H. Chamberlin

History of the Eighty-First Regiment Ohio Infantry Volunteers

During the War of the Rebellion

W. H. Chamberlin

History of the Eighty-First Regiment Ohio Infantry Volunteers
During the War of the Rebellion

ISBN/EAN: 9783337116675

Printed in Europe, USA, Canada, Australia, Japan

Cover: Foto ©ninafisch / pixelio.de

More available books at **www.hansebooks.com**

Capt Ozro J Dodds   Major W H Chamberlin
Adjutant John R Hunt Capt Charles Lane. Capt W A Johnson.

Surgeon W. H. Lamme. Lieut. Col. W. H. Hill.
Surgeon W. C. Jacobs. Brevet Brig. Gen'l R. N. Adams. Major W. Clay Henry.
Surgeon R. G. McLean. Major Frank Evans.

HISTORY

OF THE

EIGHTY-FIRST REGIMENT

OHIO INFANTRY VOLUNTEERS,

DURING THE

WAR OF THE REBELLION.

BY W. H. CHAMBERLIN,

Late Major of the Regiment.

CINCINNATI:
GAZETTE STEAM PRINTING HOUSE, COR. FOURTH & VINE STREETS.
1865.

PREFACE.

In preparing this Book it has been my aim to present the History of the Regiment as distinctly as possible, and yet to make the account of its operations intelligible to the general reader, by giving such accompanying descriptions of Battles and Campaigns as were necessary. Up to the beginning of the Savannah Campaign, I was able to obtain the facts requisite for this plan, but from that time to the close of the War, I was compelled to relinquish the general account of the movements of the rest of the Division, Corps and Army, and confine myself simply to the doings of the Eighty-First Ohio. This, however, does not detract from the interest of the story to those who passed through those Campaigns, as their own knowledge of events will serve to supplement this account.

It may be well to record here that the cost of publishing a sufficient number of copies to supply one, gratis, to each member of the Regiment serving between the dates of June 1, 1863, and January 1, 1865, was defrayed by an appropriation from the Regimental Fund.

There was no provision for the expense of portraits in the appropriation for publishing the Book; hence, inasmuch as it was suggested that they would form a desirable feature, I issued a circular to all the Officers requesting them to permit the insertion of their portraits, at their expense, and naming the lowest sum at which it could be done. The result is before the reader. No one will regret more than myself the absence of many familiar faces,—especially of the dead—but it is too late now to remedy it, and I feel that I have used every means in my power, without success.

The design of producing this little work originated in the belief that such a record, in a permanent form, would be acceptable to the living as a memento of their suffering and services in the War of the Rebellion, and that it also might serve as a slight tribute to the memory of those gallant and heroic members of our Regiment who have laid their lives upon their Country's altar.   W. H. C.

ATHENS, O., Dec. 1, 1865.

CONTENTS.

CHAPTER I.

ORGANIZATION—BATTLE OF SHILOH.

An Adopted Child.—Independent Regiment.—Under the Pathfinder.—Captain O'Kane's Company "Kidnapped."—Ohio Claims the Eighty-First.—Benton Barracks.—"Rifles at Franklin.—Hermann.—After Jeff. Jones.—Pursuit of Cobb.—Stationed.—Marching Orders.—Aboard the Meteor.—Pittsburg Landing.—Assigned to Second Brigade.—Battle of Shiloh.—Death of Captain Armstrong.—Second Days' Battle.—The 81st Takes a Battery.—Bravery of Lieutenant Post.—Victory!..........PAGE 9

CHAPTER II.

CORINTH—HAMBURG—BATTLE OF CORINTH.

General Davies and General Oglesby.—Advance on Corinth.—Skirmish.—Resignation and Promotions.—March to Boonville.—Brigade Drills.—Cutting Down a Forest.—Recruiting Party Sent North.—Hamburg.—Sergeant Howell's Adventure on Steamer Terry.—Lieutenant Irion the Last Commandant at Shiloh.—Return to Corinth.—Battle of Iuka.—Battle of Corinth.—Almost a Defeat.—Death of General Hackelman.—Brilliant Charge.—General Oglesby Wounded.—Anxious Night.—Second Day.—Rebels Defeated.—Loss of 81st Ohio.—Serg't McCall...PAGE 20

CHAPTER III.

PURSUIT OF PRICE—GARRISON DUTY.

To Bridge Creek.—Frightened Contrabands.—Night March.—Truce Party.—Return.—General Dodge.—"Massa Lied"—Arrival of Five New Companies.—Their Reception.—Drill.—How Water Was Furnished.—Festivities.—Colored Weddings.......PAGE 34

CHAPTER IV.

WINTER AT CORINTH.

Expedition to Tupelo.—Return.—Forrest Cuts the Railroad.—Half Rations.—Bliss of Ignorance.—Fruitless March.—Muddy Trip.—Night on a Barge.—Naval Expedition.—A Wheel Breaks.—Back to Corinth.—Model Camp.—Celebration of Shiloh..PAGE 47

CHAPTER V.

EXPEDITION TO TUSCUMBIA.

Fording Bear Creek.—Fight with Roddy.—Object of the Expedition.—Skirmish at "Rock Cut."—Tuscumbia Taken.—Colonel Straight Departs at Midnight.—Demonstrrtion at Town Creek.—Grand Skirmish Line.—Return to Corinth.—Summer Quarters..PAGE 51

CHAPTER VI.

POCAHONTAS AND PULASKI.

March to Pocahontas.—Terrific Storm.—Good Living.—General Oglesby's Farewell Address.—Building Winter Quarters.—Goodby "Camp Brough."—March to Pulaski, Tennessee.—Muddy Bivouac.—Lumber that Could Walk.—Milling.—Regiment Divided.—General Dodge's Plan for Foraging.—Captain Hill Superintendent of Mills..PAGE 61

CHAPTER VII.

AT PULASKI.

Little Johnny Nott Captures a Captain.—Routine of Duty.—Re-enlisting as Veterans.—To Lynnville.—Guerrilla Captures.—To Pulaski Again.—Rail Making on Martin's Plantation.—A Sudden Movement.—Military Execution ....PAGE 69

CHAPTER VIII.

ATLANTA CAMPAIGN—FROM PULASKI TO RESACA.

Anniversary of Advance on Corinth.—First Day's March.—Taking Cars.—Chickamauga.—Snake Creek Gap.—Skirmish at Resaca.—Why Resaca was not Captured.—"Johnston's Coming!"..PAGE 78

CHAPTER IX.

ATLANTA CAMPAIGN—FROM SNAKE CREEK GAP TO LAY'S FERRY.

The First Ditch.—The Union Hosts Marshaled.—Battle of Resaca.—Laying Pontoons.—Oostenaula River.—"Muslin Ships."—Who Shall Cross?—The Forlorn Hope.—"Too Late!"—Success.—Three Capture Eleven.—Close of Battle at Resaca.—Pontoons Laid.—Enemy Charge.—Color-Bearer Wounded.............PAGE 84

CHAPTER X.

ATLANTA CAMPAIGN—FROM LAY'S FERRY TO BIG SHANTY.

Battle of Rome Cross Roads.—Enemy Driven.—Colonel Burke Wounded.—Grand Race.—Johnston Stops to Fight at Etowah River—But Runs Again.—McPherson Makes a Second Flank Movement.—Van Wert.—Dallas.—Rebel Assault.—Rice's Brigade Repulses It.—Fatal Skirmishing.—Rebels Interrupt a Movement.—Night Attack.—Fire Works on a Grand Scale.—General Dodge as Ordnance Officer.—General McPherson's Tiger Hard to Let Go.—Colonel Mersey Gets Out of a Trap.—March to Acworth.—To Big Shanty..PAGE 94

CHAPTER XI.

ATLANTA CAMPAIGN—FROM BIG SHANTY TO KENNESAW MOUNTAIN.

Enemy's Watch Tower.—Skirmish Firing.—Artillery Combats.—"Old Leather Breeches."—A Picket Truce.—Unceremoniously Closed.—Rebels Fall Back.—General Sherman Going Into Marietta.—Kennesaw in His Way.—A Locomotive on Picket.—Comfortable Prospect.—Advance on the 27th of June......PAGE 109

CHAPTER XII.

ATLANTA CAMPAIGN—FROM KENNESAW MOUNTAIN TO NEAR ATLANTA.

Artillery Practice.—Soldiers' Concert.—McPherson to Make Another Flank Movement.—Kennesaw Ours!—Nickajack Creek.—Novel Celebration of July 4th.—Lieutenant Lockwood Wounded.—Battle of Ruff's Mills.—On to the Chattahoochee.—Fletcher B Haynes.—From Right to Left.—What a Dying Mule Can Do.—Hot March.—Roswell.—Fording the Chattahoochee.—Advance on Atlanta.—Decatur.—Closing In Around Atlanta......PAGE 116

CHAPTER XIII.

ATLANTA CAMPAIGN—BATTLES OF JULY 22D AND 28TH.

Hood's Stratagem.—Defeated by Accident.—Skirmishing in the Rear!—General Sweeney's Command in Line of Battle.—The Enemy!—Desperate Fighting!—Victorious Charge.—General McPherson Killed.—Fifteenth Corps Assaulted.—DeGres' Battery Taken.—Colonel Mersey's Brigade Helps to Regain It.—"Killed," Captain Charles Lane.—Lieutenant Hoover.—Colonel Mersey Parts from His Command.—To the Right.—Battle of the 28th.—Siege of Atlanta.—Resignations.—Promotions.—General Dodge Wounded.—Exploit of Corporal Harpster.......PAGE 130

CHAPTER XIV.

"ATLANTA OURS, AND FAIRLY WON."

Final Flank Movement.—Army of the Tennessee Again on the Right.—Destroying Railroad.—Contrabands Delighted.—Battle of Jonesboro.—Atlanta Taken!—To Lovejoy's.—Back to East Point.—M. R. Blizzard Died.—"A Full Month's Rest."—Muster Out of Non-veterans..................................Page 141

CHAPTER XV.

THE MARCH FROM ATLANTA TO THE SEA.

To Rome.—Left Wing 16th Army Corps Discontinued.—Promotions.—Hood Tries to Drive Sherman Northward.—Beginning of a Long Journey.—Atlanta Destroyed.—Thanksgiving Dinner in Georgia.—Palm Trees.—A Lost Brigade.—Fight at Eden.—Colonel Adams' Brigade Captures Artillery, &c.—F. B. Haynes Killed.—Fort McAllister Taken.—Daring Feat of Captain McCain, Lieutenant Pittman and Their Parties.—Into Savannah.—Feasting.—General Logan Returns..................Page 147

CHAPTER XVI.

THROUGH THE CAROLINAS TO PEACE.

To Sister's Ferry.—Entering the "Kingdom" of South Carolina.—Difficulties.—Columbia Captured.—Colonel Adams Takes Camden.—"Bummers" Have a Fight.—Terrific Explosion at Cheraw.—Respect for North Carolina Loyalty.—Battle at Bentonville.—General Sherman's Order.—Ragged Review.—Two New Companies.—Night March to Pikeville.—Raleigh.—Lee's Surrender!—Morrisville.—Johnston Surrenders!—The War Over! "Homeward March."—Mustered Out at Louisville.—Paid and Discharged at Camp Dennison.—Home.—Summary...Page 157

CHAPTER XVII.

THE RANK AND FILE OF THE EIGHTY-FIRST OHIO.

Explanation.—Field and Staff.—Changes Therein.—Original Members of Company A.—Its Casualties.—The Same of Companies B and C.—Compilation from Muster-Out Rolls of Companies D, E and F.—Original Members of Company G.—Its Casualties.—The Same of Companies H and I.—Extracts from Muster-Out Roll of Company K.—The New Companies B and C—List of Wounded..................................Page 169

HISTORY

OF THE

EIGHTY-FIRST OHIO INFANTRY VOLUNTEERS.

CHAPTER I.

ORGANIZATION—BATTLE OF SHILOH.

This regiment had an organization, which, perhaps, is unlike that of any other regiment sent into the field from Ohio. It is an adopted child of the State, not one " to the manor born."

In August, 1861, the 20th Ohio (three months' regiment) was mustered out of the service. For some reason its field officers were not appointed to re-organize it for the three years' service, as was the case with most of the other three months' regiments from Ohio. Its Colonel, however, with a portion of the Field and Staff, conceived the idea of raising an independent regiment, without the aid of the State.

At that time, General Fremont, commanding in Missouri, had undertaken the Herculean labor of not only commanding, but also of creating his army. Through his influence, the orders of the War Department were such that any one could enlist men for his army, and could have them mustered singly, or in squads, or companies, and forwarded to his headquarters at St. Louis.

With one of General Fremont's Staff officers, R. M. Corwine, of Cincinnati, Colonel Thomas Morton, formerly Colonel of the 20th Ohio, made a contract to raise a full regiment, which was to be armed with the best of rifles, and was to be known as "Morton's Independent Rifle Regiment."

The idea of independence, as well as that of carrying the best weapon—the rifle—was tempting to many. To others, the name of the Pathfinder had a peculiar charm, and they were ambitious to follow in the steps of such a leader. To most, however, the fact that they were at once transferred to the enemy's country, instead of lying for weeks at home in camp, was most acceptable, and early in September a very good basis for a regiment was collected.

By some bad management, however, one full company, that of Captain Peter O'Kane, of Eaton, Ohio, after having been sent to St. Louis, as the first fruits of the "Independent Regiment," was actually taken possession of by Colonel Crafts J. Wright, of Cincinnati, who was also organizing an independent regiment, and was incorporated into *his* regiment. This loss, together with the fact that one or two companies which were expected to join Morton's regiment were prevailed upon to go elsewhere, delayed the filling up of the regiment so that it did not seem likely that the Colonel would fulfil his contract in the time allowed.

At this juncture, State pride fortunately intervened. Colonel Morton had taken some five or six hundred men from Ohio into the United States' service, beyond the control of the State. Although no draft was then feared, and "quotas" were far more than filled, yet the State desired to have credit for all the men furnished, and to number as many regiments as her neighbors. The State was not slow, then, to accept the proposition to take the "Independent Regiment" into its fold, and give it a name.

It was numbered the Eighty-first Ohio Infantry Volunteers. It was agreed that the officers already appointed should be commissioned by the Governor, and the State authorities were pledged to use every endeavor to have the regiment filled to the maximum.

Benton Barracks was the rendezvous of all the troops sent to Fremont's Department. In the spacious quarters and ample grounds of that well known military Camp of Instruction the regiment entered on its first military duties. Drill and guard duty were the daily routine during the short time the regiment remained at that place. On the 24th of September, 1861, the detachment received marching orders, and on the following day was taken to Franklin, Missouri, on the Pacific Railroad, under command of Captain R. N. Adams, there being no field officer present. There the men received arms. Imagine the surprise and indignation of the "Rifle Regiment" when they found that they were receiving old United States muskets, for buck and ball, formerly flint locks, but now changed to percussion! But as they were assured this was but a temporary arrangement, to equip them for an emergency, the complaint was not loud. In a day or two the regiment was ordered to Hermann, Missouri, still farther west on the river and railroad. Here the regiment went into camp, and under command of Lieutenant Colonel John A. Turley, was industrious in drill, and attained a tolerable degree of skill in the evolutions. The regiment now had reached its maximum, not the legal, but the possible. Counting Captain O'Kane's company, which had been spirited away, it numbered eight companies, of which but four were full. At this time the real organization was as follows: Company B., Captain Armstrong, recruited at Lima, Allen county, Ohio; Company C., Captain Adams, recruited at Greenfield, Highland county, Ohio; Company D., Captain P. A. Tyler, recruited at Sankusky, Ottawa county, Ohio; Company E., Captain Taylor, recruited at

Lima, Allen county, Ohio; Company F., Captain Dodds, recruited at Buena Vista, Adams county, Ohio; Company G., Captain Kinsell, recruited at Mt. Gilead, Morrow county, Ohio, and Company H., Captain Hughes, recruited at Lima, Allen county, Ohio. The aggregate was nearly six hundred, exclusive of Captain O'Kane's company.

In November of that year, rumors came of a rebel force collecting in Callaway county, across the river, under one Colonel Jeff. Jones. General Prentiss, who was then at Jefferson City, ordered the 81st Ohio and the 10th Missouri, with a section of German Home Guard artillery from Hermann by railroad to St. Auberts, where a boat was in readiness to ferry across the Missouri. It required twenty-four hours to make this movement, and it was nearly dark when the crossing was completed. It was about fifteen miles from the place of crossing to the rebel camp, and the march was to be made that night. The troops were in high spirits. Elated with the novelty of the hour and the imagined victory that awaited them, they went gaily along. At daybreak the camp was neared, and a halt and rest was ordered. When the march was resumed it was but a little while until our forces entered the town of Fulton, only to learn that the rebels had broken up camp, and had dispersed, in accordance with an agreement made the previous day between Jeff. Jones and General Henderson, who was commanding State troops in that region. Nothing was left but to return, which was done, the steamer White Cloud conveying the entire force from St. Auberts to Hermann.

In December, Lieutenant-Colonel Turley's resignation was accepted, and as Major Lamison was still in Ohio, Colonel Morton was the only field officer present.

December 20, 1861, guerrillas in Northern Missouri tore up the North Missouri railroad. Orders came immediately for the force at Hermann to cross and march to the railroad for the purpose of driving out the troublesome bands. The weather was extremely cold, and there was no boat on which to cross. A day or two was frittered away in attempts to cross with skiffs. At length a ferry boat from down the river was obtained, and the crossing effected by midnight of the of 24th of December. Snow was on the ground and the weather was extremely cold, yet the troops gathered around their fires and were comfortable. The first day's march brought the force to the railroad at High Hill. That night a refugee from Danville, nine miles distant, brought word that a band of rebels under Cobb were in that town. The troops were so wearied that the Colonel thought it unwise to attempt to go there that night, yet it was necessary to keep it a secret to avoid being annoyed by voluntary applications for permission to go and attack them.

In the morning, after a reconnoisance made by Adjutant Evans and others of the 81st Ohio, it was determined to "move in force" upon Danville, the county seat of Montgomery County. It was three o'clock in the evening when the advance reached town, and learned that the rebel rear had just left. After a slight halt, during which a few mounted men had found the rebels in line of battle just outside the town, the exciting word of "fall in!" rung through the town. In a twinkling knapsacks were unslung, and a pursuit commenced. Vain, however, as the rebels were mounted, and could easily evade us. Here the regiment lost its first prisoner. Scott, of Company F., who was out as a skirmisher, and becoming lost, walked directly into the rebel camp.

We had the satisfaction of hearing, however, that we had driven the rebel force upon other troops at Silver Creek, where they were beaten and dispersed. During the next two weeks the regiment was marching through North Missouri, sleeping on the ground, in snow and sleet and rain, with no covering but the blankets carried along. At the end of that time it was stationed at Wellsville, Montgomery City, Florence and Danville, on the N. M. R. R. with headquarters at the latter place.

During the two months the regiment was thus stationed it did an enormous amount of work in scouting, arresting accomplices and principals in the work of destroying the railroad, and in restoring peace and quiet to the whole country round about.

About the 1st of March, 1862, orders were received to report to General Halleck, at St. Louis. In a few days the regiment was gathered together, and was in the city. Colonel Morton reported in person to General Halleck, and received orders to go in Barracks until his regiment could be equipped and ready for the field. Never were troops more elated than was the 81st regiment upon the receipt of that order. Being an incomplete regiment many had thought it would never be sent to the field, but would always be kept guarding railroads, or such duty. With light hearts the boys marched into Benton Barracks once more. In a day or two the hight of joy was reached by the regiment, upon receiving an order to turn over the hated old muskets, and receive new short Enfield Rifles. Scarcely was this completed until marching orders were received, and in the clear moonlight of early evening, with flashing bayonets fixed, and martial strains from its band, the 81st Ohio made a triumphal march through the city of St. Louis, and embarked on the steamer Meteor.

This was just after the successes of Grant at Forts Henry and Donelson, and at the beginning of the collection of the vast army since known as the Army of the Tennessee. Every steamer almost on the western waters was chartered by Government, conveying troops and munitions of war to the place of rendezvous for this new army.

The steamer Meteor, with excellent luck, made an easy

and quick voyage to Pittsburg Landing, arriving there at about midnight of March 17th. Colonel Morton, with almost superhuman efforts, succeeded in effecting a landing of the troops, and all stores and equipments that night, which was a fortunate thing, as, in the crowded condition of the landing at that time, troops were often compelled to remain on board the crowded and filthy boats for several days in succession.

Dull indeed was the prospect as the soldiers awoke that morning from their brief hour of sleep. A wilderness lay before them; behind, was many a weary mile back to home and civilization. As they sat on the ground in that little corn-field, afterward the Hospital ground, many a tender line was written to the far-off friends in the distant North.

Tents were soon pitched near the old army Post-office, and the regiment patiently awaited orders. As isolated regiments were arriving daily, it was several days before they could be assigned. In a few days the 81st Ohio was assigned to the Second Brigade, Second Division of the Army of the Tennessee, and removed its camp to the place assigned to its Brigade, near the right rear of that encampment. The Second Brigade was then commanded by Colonel McArthur, of the 12th Illinois, and the Second Division by General C. F. Smith. The regiment went earnestly into the duty of drilling, under the direction mostly of Adjutant Evans, and attained a proficiency that was valuable in the coming contest.

Sabbath morning of April 6, 1862, beamed brightly. Aside from flying rumors of skirmishes near the outposts, the most of the troops were entirely ignorant of the presence of an enemy. The usual morning inspection was in progress, when the sound of artillery and musketry far off to the front and left announced the opening of the battle. Orders were immediately given to fall in, and await orders. Before the regiment was in line orders came, and were to the effect that the regiment should proceed to a bridge across Snake Creek, which formed the boundary of the encampment on the right. As soon as possible the regiment was in the position assigned. Deploying a company as skirmishers, Colonel Morton quietly awaited in that deep woods the development of events. Louder and louder, and nearer were the crashing of artillery, and the continuous roar of musketry. We could only guess that our troops were being driven back—we could see nothing. At last, at nearly noon, we were withdrawn and placed in position on our own color line. The first evidences of our discomfiture came pouring in upon us in the form of straggling groups of wounded and demoralized troops from regiments that had been in action. They all told sorrowful tales of how their regiments were all cut up. It was nearly one o'clock when the 81st Ohio first saw the enemy approaching its front. It was a small cavalry force, and as our position was favorable, a volley from the two companies on the right put them to flight.

Meantime the conflict on the left was progressing, and the sound approached alarmingly near. About two o'clock there was a lull. Our line had fallen back almost as far as it could or would go. The enemy, too, seemed wary of approaching nearer. At this juncture General Grant ordered Colonel Morton to move toward the centre of our entire line of battle, and then forward until he found the enemy. The movement was cautiously made. Starting up a ravine in rear of our line, he proceeded thus for some distance, until he could go unperceived to the front, and then passed through our line of battle at a point where General Sherman was watching the movements of the enemy. Passing in a diagonal direction toward the front and left, the Colonel soon found his little regiment alone far in advance of our main line, and entirely out of sight of it. The ground was nearly level, but it was a forest, and covered more or less with undergrowth. As the left of the regiment (it was marching by flank, left in front,) emerged into a clear piece of ground, it was suddenly greeted with a discharge of canister from a battery not more than two hundred yards away. It was directed, no doubt, at the Colonel and his party, who were riding in advance of the regiment. One of the Orderlies was severely wounded, and was left. He belonged to the 4th U. S. Cavalry. The regiment immediately formed line "faced to the rear," and lying down delivered a volley or two which had the effect of silencing the enemy's fire. Evidently our little force perplexed the rebel commander, and he wanted time to ascertain our intentions. Lying there we could distinctly see the interminable lines of the enemy, dotted with their banners, and waiting for orders. Not liking our position, Colonel Morton ordered a movement a little farther to the left, in a little ravine. To do this a road, swept by the enemy's battery at short range, had to be passed. A company at a time ran the gauntlet, and thus the whole regiment was safely re-formed in the ravine. While in this position a cavalry force of the enonemy commenced a movement to get behind our left, but before it was completed, General Grant ordered the regiment back to the main lines. As this movement was begun the enemy opened again with grape and canister, and just as Captain Martin Armstrong, who commanded the right company, gave the command, " by file right, *march !*" a grape shot struck him in the head and killed him instantly. His Orderly Sergeant caught him in his arms and bore him from the field. The regiment was extricated without further loss, and upon reporting to General Grant, Colonel Morton was complimented upon having foiled the enemy and kept him in check until our main line could be firmly established. He was then ordered to take a place in line again, near the right. Before this was completed, the famous artillery duel, with which the first day ended, was commenced. Taking position in line where it then was, the regiment lay with anxious suspense, listening to the unearthly screams of the shells flying over or bursting near them.

Night brought silence, except the regular booming of the huge guns of the gunboats, but it brought no rest except what the wearied soldiers could gain on the hard damp ground.

Morning of April 7th found the Army of the Tennessee in line, re-assured by the timely arrival of Buell's army, and ready for the signal to advance.

The Second Division, to which the 81st Ohio belonged, had suffered extremely the first day. Its commander, General W. H. L. Wallace, (General Smith being too unwell to take the field,) had been killed, and Colonel Tuttle, 2nd Iowa, had assumed command. He was wounded, leaving the command to Colonel McArthur, 12th Illinois.

The regiments had become scattered during the day and night, and there being no time for regular organization, provisional brigades were appointed. Colonel Morton was appointed to the command of one of these.

The advance was a grand sight. To the right and left, as far as the eye could reach, could be seen the blue lines of the Federal army, displaying the bright colors of the Stars and Stripes in beautiful contrast with the dull leaden hue of the yet unclothed trees. There was a mile of marching before the enemy was found, although other portions of the line were engaged. At last, after crossing an open field, the 81st Ohio took position in a little ravine, and was surprised to find a rude breastwork of logs, manned by the enemy, and completely raking the regiment from left to right. The rebels were not slow to open fire, and when it was discovered, and, that the shell and shot from two opposite batteries were also flying through our ranks, it was determined to withdraw. Owing to the favorable nature of the ground, this was done with but small loss. It was in this movement that the second member of the regiment fell, private Wm. Mc. Adams, of Company C.

As a portion of the Provisional brigade was then engaged, and as Colonel Morton was provided with neither Staff nor Orderlies, he relinquished his brigade and took charge of the regiment. The action at that time had become so general and so close, that it was but a short time until the 81st Ohio found itself again alone, and closely confronting a rebel force. Lying down, the eager boys opened a brisk fire, which was as hotly returned by the enemy. In the crash of musketry and the rattle of the balls there was engendered a kind of fierce frenzy which prevented the falling here and there of a comrade from causing a single heart to quail. So furiously did our brave boys ply the rebels with their cold lead that at last they broke and fled. No sooner was this perceived than the 81st rose, and with yells that spoke their first feeling of victory, followed the vanquished foe. So wild was their enthusiasm that they never halted or paused until they had gone far in advance of any support, and suddenly found themselves flanked by both artillery and infantry. Even then it was with difficulty that they were withdrawn. In this charge the little regiment had captured a rebel battery, and killed all the horses. It had also captured a number of prisoners. It was here that its principal loss was sustained. Lieutenant Post, while gallantly cheering on his men, was mortally wounded, and many others were killed and wounded.

It was now about the close of the struggle. Discomfited, the rebels sullenly withdrew, and left General Grant master of the field. Rest, and caring for the dead and wounded occupied the next day. Then came nearly a month of inactivity, during which General Halleck arrived and assumed command. Re-organization and reinforcements made it soon the largest army that had yet been collected during the war.

CHAPTER II.

CORINTH—HAMBURG—BATTLE OF CORINTH.

Brigadier-General T. A. Davies was appointed commander of the Second Division, and Brigadier-General R. J. Oglesby appointed to the command of the 2d Brigade, which included the 81st Ohio.

On the 29th of April the 2d Division started toward Corinth. Early in May it took its position beyond Monterey, in the grand line of approach formed by General Halleck. It was the third division in the line, counting from the right. Sherman was on the extreme right, then Hurlbut, then Davies, then the right division of Buell's army. In Davies' division the 81st Ohio occupied the left of the 2d Brigade—the 3d Brigade being between it and Buell's force.

There was nothing of importance occurred in this advance, except that on the 21st of May, when a general advance was ordered, the 81st participated in the very considerable skirmish which ensued, and lost several wounded.

Major Lamison resigned immediately after the battle of Shiloh, on account of ill-health. In May the Governor appointed Captain Robert N. Adams Lieutenant-Colonel, *vice* Turley, and Adjutant Frank Evans, Major, *vice* Lamison. Major Evans immediately entered upon his duties, but Colonel Adams was absent, sick, and did not return until August.

After the evacuation of Corinth, the 2d Division participated in the pursuit, going as far as Boonville. Taking into consideration the condition of the troops, from their constant watching for a month, and the fact that the heat was intense, that march to Boonville and return to Corinth was the most severe the regiment ever performed. It was with a grateful sense of relief that the weary men encamped near Corinth on the 12th of June, with a prospect of rest.

The life of a soldier, although often styled lazy, is never one of rest. To sustain dicipline, to preserve health, and to insure safety, there is a necessity for constant watchfulness, so that to many, a campaign is preferable to garrison duty. In this instance the rest was little more than the privilege of keeping camp in one place. General Davies, the Division Commander, went North on sick leave. General Oglesby relinquished command of the 2d Brigade to assume command of the Division, and Colonel Crafts J. Wright, 22d Ohio, took command of the Brigade. He insisted on the most industrious drills, himself taking charge of brigade drills, that began at daylight, before breakfast, and continued until eight or nine o'clock, by which time both officers and men would be well nigh exhausted. How many a poor soldier of the 2d Brigade has reason to thank the surgeons who interfered to have this well-intended, but mistaken system of drills abolished! Then there was the picket duty—the interminable details for fatigue duty, and the forage details, and the Sunday afternoon brigade dress parade, with its three hours slow ceremony—all these combined to make the rest merely nominal.

In this condition of affairs, about the middle of July the 81st Ohio was detailed to work on the grand chain of fortifications which General Halleck began to build around Corinth. Beginning at the Kossuth road, on the southwest, it had the duty assigned it of felling the timber to form abatis in front of the line. The timber was very heavy—the weather oppressively hot, and of course, the duty was no light one. But the "boys" understood how to make work light, and as the adjoining fields furnished an ample supply of green corn, and the orchards yielded peaches and apples, they were contented and healthy. For some reason not now remembered, the supply of clothing was exhausted about that time, and the men were in a condition of raggedness never equaled before or since. They often spoke of the appropriateness of that kind of backwoods service under the circumstances. By the middle of August the regiment had felled a belt of timber three hundred yards in width, and extending from the Kossuth Road to the Memphis railroad—a distance of about four miles. It made a mark there which centuries can not efface.

In July of this year, by order of General Halleck, a recruiting party, consisting of Quartermaster Adams, Lieutenant W. C. Henry, and Sergeants Darling, Johnson and Pittman, was sent to Ohio with authority to obtain enough recruits to fill up the regiment. To this end, Company H. was discontinued and its members assigned to Company E. Company G. was in like manner consolidated with Company F. This made five minimum companies in the regiment.

About the middle of August the 81st Ohio was ordered to Hamburg, on the Tennessee river. It marched there in an afternoon and morning. The object of sending it was to relieve the 14th Wisconsin, which was there on duty, and to guard the public stores at that place until they could be removed. The place was about to be given up. Colonel Morton assumed command of the post. Lieutenant-Colonel Adams was made Provost Marshal, and Major Evans was left in command of the regiment. The month spent at Hamburg was a happy and eventful one. A little mounted force was organized, which, under command of Lieutenant Corns, scoured the country effectually, and brought grief to the guerrillas who lurked in that locality. A detail of ten or twelve men, under Sergeant Howell, was ordered down the river from Hamburg, on board the steamer Terry, as a guard for it, to Paducah. A gunboat also accompanied as a convoy. The Terry had aboard two steel Wiard guns to aid in her protection.

The downward trip was successfully made. On the return, while the Terry was lying by one night, near the mouth of Duck River, with a few pickets on shore, Napier, with a heterogeneous rabble of troops, guerrillas and citizens made a descent on the boat, dispersed the pickets before they could reach the landing—captured the boat and entire crew, including several of the men of the 81st Ohio. The gunboat was not at hand to render assistance. The guns and whatever else of value was on the boat was then taken off; and the Terry was consigned to the flames. The pickets, four or five in number, who were cut off from the boat, seeing the capture, determined to make the best of their way back to Hamburg. Casting their guns and accouterments into the Tennessee River, they wandered along as best they could up the river until they found a man whom they ventured to trust with the truth of their situation. They happened to open their case to a Union man, and he directed them to Lexington, on the Corinth and Columbus railroad, whence they reached Corinth by rail and marched to Hamburg.

While at Hamburg the Provost Marshal's office was crowded with citizens flocking in from the neighboring counties to take the oath. Colonel Adams was constantly employed in this business. Lieutenant Irion, who, with a detachment of about twenty men occupied Pittsburg Landing, was also Provost Marshal, and had his hands full of work in swearing the citizens who were eager to be numbered with the loyal. This was the last military occupation of that classic field of blood—Shiloh battle-field.

Long will the members of the 81st remember with pleasure their brief month at Hamburg. The vegetables that made their tables groan—the luscious fruits and melons that were theirs in abundance—the rare fish that leaped from the Tennessee—the rarer sport of bathing in that noble river—all these luxuries of a soldiers' life, their later experience taught them to remember and appreciate.

About the middle of September the order came to evacuate Hamburg, and return to Corinth. All the public stores had been removed; only one little steamer remained. This, by order of General Grant, was scuttled and sunk at the landing. About this time the enemy began to make bolder movements against us. Buell was about beginning his famous retrograde movement toward Louisville. Scarcely had we reached Corinth until the evacuation of Iuka began. The 81st was stationed on the east of Corinth and picketed the roads leading to Iuka. Well do some of us remember the frightened movements of the cavalry from Iuka, as they chassezed in and out of Corinth for one or two days. And we remember, too, the long, dark lines of contrabands, running for freedom and life into the city of refuge—Corinth.

It was but a few days until orders were received to march. General Ord, then commanding the District of Corinth, took command of the body of troops that moved from Corinth on this expedition. General Grant himself accompanied General Ord's column. General Rosecrans moved on Iuka from Rienzi and vicinity by way of Jacinto, expecting to take the rebel force, then occupying Iuka, in rear. General Ord moved to Burnsville, and there rested, waiting for Rosecrans to get up before he pressed against Price. He waited too long, however, as Rosecrans pushed on and fought the battle of Iuka alone. General Ord's column returned to Corinth, and the 2d Brigade took up camp in its old position, two miles south of Corinth, on the Mobile railroad, at a place known to us as the "Brigade Camp."

Gen. Davies had, before this, returned to the command of the division, and Gen. Oglesby, the idol of his men, had resumed command of his old brigade.

On Thursday evening, Oct. 2d, orders were issued to be ready to move at a moment's notice. At 3 A. M. Gen. Oglesby's brigade was formed on the color line, but rested until after daylight, when it, with the remainder of the division, marched off toward Corinth. Immediately after the battle of Iuka, Gen. Grant had removed his headquarters to Jackson, Tenn., and Gen. Ord had been relieved by Gen. Rosecrans. This left Gen. Rosecrans commander of all the troops in the district of Corinth, consisting of two divisions of Gen. Pope's old Army of the Mississippi and the 2d and 6th Divisions of the Army of the Tennessee. Gen. Rosecrans had concentrated his whole army within reach of Corinth, and was ready for the blow which was about to fall.

But as my narrative will hardly justify me in going beyond the brigade, I return to it, where we left it, marching toward Corinth on the eventful morning of the 3d of October, 1862. When half way to the town, artillery was distinctly heard to the northwest. It was the first intimation to many that a battle was to be fought. The rebels, after Iuka, had apparently never halted, but kept right on through Tupelo and Ripley to Pocahontas, and following the Memphis & Charleston Railroad, were approaching Corinth from the northwest.

As Gen. Oglesby entered the town, it was evident that something was going to happen. Troops were moving in every direction, teams were driving at break-neck speed, and all the usual business appearance of the town was giving way to inextricable confusion. At the same time, the sound of artillery grew more distinct and nearer, and orderlies and staff officers were dashing by "on hurried hoof." Soon Gen. Davies' division marched out by Battery

Robinett, on the north side of the Memphis & Charleston Railroad. Going but a short distance into the timber, it was halted, and here a stream of the superfluities of the outer camps in that direction passed us, going in to Corinth. It was evident that the battle had reached the position of our outposts. Here and there a wounded man passed by. Col. Baldwin, with the 3d Brigade, was sent off to the left, and took position where the old line of rebel works touch the M. & C. R. R., about three miles from Corinth. The 2d Brigade went into the rebel works a half mile further to the right, while the 1st Brigade was on its right. The line, thus partially covered by but little over two thousand men, was nearly two miles in length.

The regiments were stretched to their utmost capacity, in a thin line, but yet there were immense gaps which could not be filled. The 81st Ohio was placed on the left of the brigade, then a section of artillery just at the angle of the works, next the 12th Illinois, and on the right the 9th Illinois. An old abatis, formed by felling the timber for the space of three hundred yards in front of the works, had lost much of its strength by time, it having been made by the rebels before our occupation of the place. Beyond this was thick woods, whose abundant foliage, yet unhurt by the frost, formed an impenetrable cover for the movements of the rebel troops. Hardly had the troops of the 1st and 2d Brigades got into position until it was manifest that they were not a moment too soon. Every now and then a rebel officer would ride out of the woods to take a view of our defenses, and it was evident that they were marshaling for a charge upon our works. Opposite the salient angle where a section of our artillery was posted, between the 12th Illinois and 81st Ohio, was a little eminence. On this the rebels placed two guns, and announced their presence by a discharge of canister at our lines. Our battery replied vigorously and with great bravery, in a very exposed position; but with unlooked for impetuosity, the rebels, in overwhelming numbers, rushed from their cover into the abatis, and with demoniac yells moved upon our weak line. The crash and rattle and din that followed was like the struggle of two great monsters, terrific but brief. In five minutes from the time the rebels emerged from the woods, they had pierced our line, captured several pieces of artillery and driven us from our works. Driven but not defeated, the gallant Oglesby immediately, with all the might of his earnest mind, set to work to rally his command. The result was that, with a victorious foe close on our heels, we were reformed not far from the line we had left—shattered and broken, it is true, and missing many brave men, but yet resolved to "do or die." Gen. Oglesby addressed a few cheering words to his broken column, and a new life seemed infused into every soldier. It was a sure harbinger of victory to come.

The 1st Brigade had also been compelled to withdraw, at the same time, from its position on the right, and the 3d Brigade, away off on the left, was nearly cut off, but succeeded finally in getting back to the position of the rest of the division. The troops evidently now had to be concentrated. A new line was formed in front of the "White House," which, while forming, was furiously assailed by two batteries of the enemy, placed in close proximity to our lines. Our own batteries replied with spirit for some time, when they were ordered to withdraw. At the same time, our infantry was withdrawn to a line a short distance to the rear, running between the White House and Corinth. The rebels confidently pressed on, but our lines now being compact and without gaps as before, we maintained our position with firmness. On, on came the rebels, our troops, lying close to the ground, were unhurt by the rebel balls. It was here, while close behind the 81st Ohio, that the gallant Gen. P. A. Hackelman, of Indiana, was mortally wounded. As he fell from his horse, he was caught by Private C. P. McClelland, and Major Evans of the 81st Ohio, and such care given him as the circumstances allowed. All at once, as if by magic, the long line arose, nerved to action by the sight of this beloved, dying General, and with cheers that spoke the determination of their hearts, every man sprang forward! Forward, borne by brave hearted men, sped the bright banners of every regiment. It was a grand sight! In the hottest of the fray could be seen the now exultant Oglesby riding up and down the lines of his brigade, hat in hand, cheering, laughing and weeping for joy as he saw the complete victory won now by his brigade and the others, which only a few hours before had been almost disgraced by defeat. Poor man! just as the charge of our troops was about ended, by driving the rebels back upon their reserves, he fell severely wounded. Our troops were now recalled, and the day's battle was ended. So furious had been our last charge that the rebels did not venture another attack that night. In this day's fighting the brunt of the battle fell upon Gen. Davies' division, and it is now incontestible that but for the gallant stand and the brilliant charge made by this division at the White House, on that afternoon of the 3d of October, the town of Corinth, with its valuable stores and artillery, would have fallen into rebel hands.

That was an anxious night. The events of the day had developed the fact that the enemy far outnumbered us. We had already lost heavily in the day's battle. The fortifications of the place were merely nominal; not a foot of intrenchments for infantry was there; all the work in that direction had been expended in erecting works for the artillery, and even this was not complete. Battery Richardson, which played a conspicuous part in the struggle of the next day, was built by the contrabands during the day and night of the 3d, the negroes digging for dear life while a portion of the battle of the 3d was being fought in their presence.

At the Tishomingo Hotel, which had been converted into a hospital, there was sad evidence of the severity of the trial through which the 2d Division (Davies') had passed that day. Every room was filled with the wounded, and the porches were also crowded, mostly from Davies' division. In the little room at the end of the lower porch, designated the ladies' parlor, could be seen the three brigade commanders of Gen. Davies' division—Col. Baldwin, slightly wounded; Gen. Oglesby, suffering intensely from his wound, which the surgeons hardly dared say was not mortal; and Gen. P. A. Hackelman, who was dying. His wound was by a musket ball through the neck, evidently aimed directly at him, as he was prominent, being on horseback.

There was but little rest that night for the Union troops. Stanley's division, which had only been represented by a brigade in a portion of the battle of the 3d, was now brought up and posted, covering Batteries Williams and Robinett, between the Memphis & Charleston and Columbus Railroads. On his left was placed McKean, whose division had been well represented by McArthur's brigade during the day. Gen. Davies' division was placed next, facing northwardly, its left resting on Battery Powell and its right covering Battery Richardson. On his right, in *echelon*, was Hamilton's strong divison, which had as yet scarcely been engaged. Almost all the night was occupied by these movements, so that the wearied soldiers scarcely had an hour's sleep after their almost superhuman exertions of the day. Gen. Rosecrans himself did not retire until 3 A. M., and it was daylight before all the troops were in position.

Scarcely had day dawned until the sound of artillery and the explosion of shell in the town of Corinth, told us that the enemy had been watchful, too, and had made a bold advance. Our siege guns and light artillery replied so effectively that the support of the rebel battery was driven away, and our skirmish line advancing, it captured the two guns and the Captain in command. This battery, however, struck several buildings in Corinth before it was silenced, carrying dismay and consternation to the inhabitants and the contrabands who occupied that locality. The wounded were hastily removed without injury, except one poor fellow who was struck by a shell and instantly killed while being carried down the stairway of the Tishomingo Hotel.

After this demonstration there was a significant lull. Many surmised that the rebels were drawing off, while others thought they were preparing for an assault. The latter supposition proved to be true. About 9 or 10 o'clock the storm broke in fury full upon Davies' devoted command. Stretched in a single line, with no reserves and no intrenchments, the wearied troops yielded before the impetuous onset of the rebels. Cheered by their apparently easy victory, Price's vagabonds rushed boldly on, hoping to make a lodgment in the town. But in this they were disappointed. Hamilton's artillery and infantry poured death into one flank; the ponderous siege guns and lighter pieces of batteries Williams and Robinett threw their deadly iron hail into the other flank, while Davies' division, rallying, turned upon their pursuers, and hurling destruction upon their front, almost literally annihilated them. A few stragglers sought safety in flight, but the greater portion of the assaulting column was made prisoners, or lay dead or wounded on the field. A feeble attempt at a second charge was made, but abortively failed. This was the end of the battle on the right. Simultaneously with their attack here, another was intended to have been made on the left; but owing to the almost impassable ground in front of our lines there, the rebels were delayed, and the first attempt had been made and had failed before the troops on the left were in readiness to attack. There, as on the right, the rebels rushed madly to death, but the ground being much less favorable, their success was not so great. They broke no portion of our line, although piles of their dead lay under the very guns of Battery Robinett. It was here that the recklessly gallant Col. Rogers, of the 2d Texas, fell while attempting to scale the parapet. He was buried in a separate grave, just where he fell—a magnanimous tribute to the bravery of an enemy.

Murderously foiled in all his attempts to capture Corinth, Price led away his remaining troops, retreating as he came by way of Pocahontas. It was near noon of the 4th when the fighting had ceased, and the fact of his retreat became known. Cheer after cheer went up from all parts of the field as General Rosecrans rode over the field and announced the result, and gave orders for a hurried pursuit.

Our losses, though great, especially in the first day's fight, did not compare with those of the enemy, most of whose dead and wounded fell into our hands. General Rosecrans, in his official report, says the rebel loss was 1,423 officers and men killed, 5,692 wounded, and 2,248 prisoners, among whom were 137 field officers, captains and subalterns, representing fifty-three regiments of infantry, sixteen of cavalry, thirteen batteries of artillery, and seven battalions. We captured also 14 stands of colors, two pieces of artillery, 3,300 stands of small arms, 4,500 rounds of ammunition and a large amount of accouterments. Our loss was 315 killed, 1,812 wounded, and 232 prisoners and missing.

The following extract from the farewell address of General Davies, on taking leave of his division, on the 25th of October following the battle, will, when compared with the above figures, tell how his division responded to the demands made on it during this battle.

* * * * * * *

"The 3d was a trying day for us, and at 2 o'clock, 1,785 officers and men of this Division had to meet the army of Van Dorn and Price at the White House. The thunder of our artillery and the rattle of our musketry bespoke a contest seldom equaled in stubbornness on both sides. Once we repulsed them with leaden hail, once with the bayonet, and once and last with pure obstinacy, and victory perched upon our banners.

"*Worn and exhausted, but never tired of doing duty*, the Division was again attacked on the 4th, and again our victorious flag waved over the heaps of rebel slain, resulting in casualties to us of 1,004, capturing 1,046 prisoners, and ten stands of the enemies' colors."

* * * * * * *

The loss of the 81st Ohio in this battle was as follows:

COMPANY B., CAPTAIN J. W. TITUS COMMANDING.

KILLED.—First Sergeant, John Johnson; Corporal Abraham Fulmer; Privates William Rankins, G. H. Adgate, John Armour.

WOUNDED.—First Lieut. James H. Corns; Sergeant Gideon Ditto; Corporals Hiram Robbins, F. Downs, F. M. Hartshorn; Privates John Linton, Christian Lehman, George Truesdale, W. D. Cunningham, M. Richards, B. Franklin, Thomas Shaw Isaac Lehman, W. F. Maltbie, Isaac McGrady, Wm. Woley.

COMPANY C., FIRST LIEUT. W. H. CHAMBERLIN COMMANDING.

KILLED.—None.

WOUNDED.—Sergeants W. H. Scroggs, Charles Depoy, Wm. W. Merrill; Privates Calvin P. McClelland, James W. Cowman, Albert Kinnamon.

Wounded and missing, Private Amos Swartz, (never since heard from.)

COMPANY D., CAPTAIN P. A. TYLER COMMANDING.

KILLED.—Corporal Henry Hardly; Privates Caleb Fogle, John F. Rose.

WOUNDED.—Sergeant W. D. Tyler, Privates Hugh L. Carlisle, John V. Bushong, Charles S. Keys, William Davis, M. W. Kimmel.

COMPANY E., FIRST LIEUT. JOHN L. HUGHES COMMANDING.

KILLED.—None.

WOUNDED.—Corporal Philip Hoot; Privates William Grant, James W. Bailey, James F. M'Ginnis, George Keith, Lewis Swearingen, Alvero Curtis.

COMPANY F., CAPTAIN OZRO J. DODDS COMMANDING.

KILLED.—Corporal Abner McCall; Privates Daniel H. Brown, L. P. Gifford.

WOUNDED.—Sergeant David McCall, mortally; Corporal Ira Hartwell; Privates George Easter, John Ford, Marcus Newland, George Crowl, John Hayslip, W. H. McCandless.

MISSING.—John P. Porter, S. Corwin.

Total, 11 killed, 44 wounded, 3 missing.

When the 81st Ohio advanced on Saturday morning, the 4th, to meet the foe, Sergeant David McCall, its color bearer, was the first to fall. He was mortally wounded by a musket ball in the abdomen. At Pittsburg Landing, although unable for duty, rising from a sick bed, he, unscathed, bravely carried our flag through those two terrible days. As soon, however, as the excitement of that conflict was over, he was taken seriously sick, and was sent North, where he lay for a long time while his life was despaired of. But he finally recovered, and returned to his regiment but a short time before this battle. He was a brave man, and fell while bearing his flag forward. Long will his memory live in the hearts of his comrades.

CHAPTER III.

PURSUIT OF PRICE AND GARRISON DUTY.

As General Rosecrans intimated, the whole army moved in pursuit on Sunday Morning—McPherson's Brigade, which had arrived the previous day, just after the battle, taking the advance. The 81st Ohio was so near the last of the column that it was delayed greatly, and at four P. M., it was hardly four miles from Corinth. At this point an order was received detaching it, and sending it to hold a bridge on Bridge Creek, southwest of Corinth, where it was reported a force of rebel cavalry was about to cross. The march of nearly six miles was made in forced time, and many members of the regiment can remember its severity. The weather was dry and unusually warm, the roads were very dusty, and water was not to be obtained. Never, perhaps, did the boys so gladly greet a stream as they did Bridge Creek on reaching it that evening. No rebels, however, were found in that vicinity, and the command rested undisturbed. That evening a little guerrilla force made an attack on the camp of our division below Corinth, which was then occupied only by convalescents and non-combatants. The scene was described as intensely ludicrous, as the flight of the frightened contrabands, and others, to Corinth was in progress. However, a few of the abler bodied soldiers formed, and with a little show of resistance, drove the invaders off, killing several of them. One who was killed was well known to many of our soldiers, lived but a mile or two away, had often been in camp, and had his oath of allegiance to the Government of the United States in his pocket at the time he was shot.

The 81st remained two or three days on Bridge Creek, and then was ordered into its old camp. To those who have been suddenly called away from a comfortable camp, such as ours was there, and who have spent a week in battle and marching, not to mention partial fasting and loss of sleep, it may well be supposed that the prospect of return and rest was cheering. But the soldier has no right to indulge in the illusions of hope. Scarcely had the men consigned themselves to the first hour's sleep in their tents, until orders came to march immediately. By ten o'clock the march was begun, and all that weary night the poor soldiers trudged along without rest. At daylight the regiment reached its destination, which was a position on the Tuscumbia River, near Chewalla. It was considered necessary to guard that point. Just after reaching our position that morning, and stationing guards, the wearied men threw themselves on the ground and fell into a deep slumber. Most of them were shortly afterward aroused by the appearance of about three hundred rebels under flag of truce. The following extract from a letter written at that time tells of this event:

"I had just entered the dominions of the sleepy god, when a guard, out of breath, touched me on the shoulder and said that there were some men that looked like rebels trying to cross the river, but they had no guns. On repairing to the place I found a white flag flying, and discovered that the party, numbering over three hundred, constituted a force which Van Dorn had sent back, requesting permission to bury their dead. They had reached Chewalla on Sunday, where they were detained by General Rosecrans until Thursday, when they were sent beyond our lines, with an apology for having detained them so long, and an assurance that their dead were already decently interred.

"The rebel army having burned the bridge at this place, they were detained an hour or two in making a passable ford by which they could get their three wagons across. This interval was industriously improved by our soldiers in the exchange of news, sentiment, canteens and money. It was a novel sight to see the soldiers of opposite armies mingling together peaceably—the men who, but a few days before, had met in deadly array on the field of battle. But there was no hatred between them. Principles, and not men, are our enemies. I talked with a number of these rebels, mostly on the subject of the Corinth battle. They accorded to us, universally, great bravery, while they were all confident that they would have succeeded if Van Dorn had not been their commander. There was no limit to their disgust against him. Colonel Berry, of the 35th Mississippi, was in command of the party. He is said to be a Missourian, from Pike or Hancock county. A chaplain, Rev. G. W. Rogers, from Liberty, Boone county, Mo., bore their flag for them.

"The conduct of the men was faultless, but their appearance was far from prepossessing. Our private soldiers are dressed far better than their colonels. I saw two of their men wearing shirts made of damask which had evidently done duty, at some time, as window curtains. Hats and caps of all shapes, sizes and colors, made them appear as widely different as possible. The only thing which they had in common was dirt. So far as this could do it, they were uniformed. When they had effected a crossing, and had re-packed their three days' rations, which General Rosecrans had issued to them, in consideration of having delayed them, they took their way toward their Southern camp-fires, first bidding us a kind and friendly farewell ' till we met again.' May it ever be our fortune to meet foes as brave and as honorable!"

The regiment remained nearly a week in this sylvan solitude, with no kind of disturbance. The neighboring farms were laid under contribution by the soldiers, and yielded abundant supplies of sweet potatoes, pork, turkeys, &c. When the pursuit of the flying army was stopped, our regiment was ordered back to Corinth, and went into a new camp within half a mile of the town. Thus ended what was then one of the most complete victories of the war. Van Dorn, having chosen his own time, place, manner of attack, and number of troops, not only failed in his assault, but was so sorely pressed on his retreat that he barely escaped with a pitiful remnant of his army.

Thus was the character of Western troops again shown to be worthy of honor, and their invincibility was established.

The remainder of this month of October, and the following November, was spent by the 81st in garrison. While Grant's main army was moving down through central Mississippi, this post was held by the troops under General G. M. Dodge, who succeeded General Davies. The duty was the ordinary garrison duty. Guerrillas and small parties of the enemy's cavalry hovered about us, making it a matter of interest and of a little danger to venture out of our lines. The railroads being unable to furnish a sufficient amount of forage for the animals of the army at Corinth, the troops were kept continually on forage expeditions, until there was not any corn of any consequence within a space of twenty-five miles in diameter about Corinth.

Contrabands kept coming in in numerous bands. I remember seeing one day a squad of twenty, who had come from about Guntown--about forty miles distant. I asked them if they knew that Massa Lincoln was going to make them all free next New Year's. They had not heard the news of the Emancipation proclamation, but they did know that freedom could be obtained at Corinth. Says one of them: "Massa tole us dat you all Yankees at Corinth would make we 'uns work on de big forts tell we died, an' den give us some beef on a cracker, an' throw in a hole alive an' bury us!"

"Why did you come here, then?"

"Oh, we knowed massa *lied!*"

On the evening of October 19th, the five new companies arrived, which had been organized in Ohio, as the result of the labors of the recruiting party consisting of Lieutenants Adams and Henry, and Sergeants Darling, Johnson and Pittman, sent North in July. It will be remembered that the old troops of the regiment had been organized previously into five companies. These recruits filled up the vacancy, and made the 81st at last a full regiment. These five companies were lettered A, G, H, I and K. Company A was organized in Allen county, Ohio, by Captain Hill, Lieut. Van Pelt and Lieut. Shaffer; Company G also in Allen and Putnam counties, by Captain Overmyer, Lieut. Sprague and Lieutenant Ferguson; Company H was organized in Adams and Scioto counties, by Lieut. Henry, Lieut. Guthrie and Lieut. Roney, and Lieut. Henry was made Captain; Company I was organized in Greenfield, Ohio, from Ross, Highland and Fayette counties, by Captain Gibson, Lieut. Robinson and Lieut. Crawford, and Company K at Galion, Crawford county, Ohio, by Captain Matthias, Lieut. Lane and Lieut. Hoover. The success of this recruiting party was beyond the most sanguine expectations. The 81st was now one of the largest regiments in the service, and the excellent quality of the men and officers composing this new accession promised well for the future.

The reception of these recruits was made a formal matter. They slept all night at the depot, having arrived late. In the morning the old troops were formed and started toward Corinth with drums beating and colors flying. When they had proceeded far enough they were halted, formed in line in open order and faced inward. The new recruits now approached, marching by the right flank, and led by Colonel Morton. As soon as the head of the column entered between the lines of the old troops they saluted their new brethren by a "present arms." When the new companies had passed entirely through, they were formed as the old troops had been, and the latter passed through their lines, in turn receiving a salute. When this was done, the whole regiment formed on the color line, and stacked arms. Then there was a looking for friends, for nearly every member of the old companies had some friend or relative in the new arrival. The same day some eighty recruits, in addition to the five full companies, were equally divided between the five old companies. The regiment was now fully organized, and the companies assigned their places in line as follows, which position was ever after adhered to. Beginning at the right, was Company B, next Company A, Company F, Company H, Company E, Company G, Company D, Company K, Company I, and on the left Company C. Thus not only old and new troops were judiciously intermingled, but also companies from the same localities were, as far as possible, placed in proximity. The next few weeks were spent in most assiduous company and battalion drill, the latter under direction of Lieutenant-Colonel Adams. The recruits learned rapidly, and very soon it would have puzzled a stranger to distinguish them by their movements from the older soldiers.

On the 1st of November, the regiment was ordered to remove to a position within the inner defenses of Corinth. It was placed on a part of the old battle-field, and prepared for a winter's stay. Winter quarters were constructed by raising the tents a few feet from the ground, making a closed wall under them of timber, and building a chimney, with old-fashioned fire-place to warm them.

An engineer force, consisting mostly of contrabands, was set to work soon after the battle of Corinth, and the result was that Corinth soon became literally a walled city. The excellent earth-works did not, of course, form an unbroken circle, but the town was enclosed by them, while on every prominent point of ground a well-constructed fort commanded the approaches. The characteristics of the works were neatness and strength. They were made under the superintendence of Captains Prime and Cossak, U. S. Topographical Engineers.

The want of water was so seriously felt, that the authorities determined to obtain it by making wells. This required a peculiar process. Three negroes, a mule, a few pullies with their ropes and tackle, and the simple auger could sink a well in a short time. The soil was so free from sand and gravel that it could be bored as easily as so much wood. An auger of three inches in diameter was first used, and afterward one of eight or nine inches, which is the final diameter of the well, exclusive of tubing. The mule, harnessed to a huge clevis-like piece of timber, which enclosed its body, and was fastened over its head at the end of a horizontal lever, raised the auger by walking around in a little circle, and thus winding the rope to which the auger was suspended, around an upright cylinder. When it was necessary to unwind, the driver gave the command "halt!" and the mule would stop; "turn!" and the mule would turn in his tracks, the clevis being made so as to turn where it connected with the lever. The auger was sunk into the earth by the men, the mule only serving to draw it up. When the boring was completed, often at a depth of one hundred feet, a tubing of plank was put down to keep the wall from crumbling in. The water was drawn by long cylindrical buckets, open at the top and having a valve at the bottom opening upward. As it sank into the water the valve opened and it was filled; of course when it was drawn up the valve would shut down and keep it full. Almost every regiment had one of these wells bored for its accommodation—all done by the same mule and negroes who had enjoyed the monopoly of well-boring about Corinth for a number of years.

To show how the dull days and long nights of winter were made subservient to the enjoyment of our troops while in garrison, in that unprepossessing little town of Corinth, I introduce here an account of some of the amusements, written at the time.

It is with a feeling akin to local pride that I announce that the festive season for the city of Corinth has actually opened. To say nothing of numerous private balls, held and attended by the indefatigable dancing descendents of Ham, the enterprise of some of the leading inhabitants has culminated in a full-blown theater—manned and equipped (pardon the nauti-military expression, *stocked* is, I believe, the professional term,) wholly by *home* talent. Last night the military, and other denizens of Corinth, were treated to the opening performance of the Hospital Troupe. The actors were all high privates, mostly from those detailed on duty at the post hospital. The proceeds of the entertainment go for the benefit of the sick. The theater, used recently as a vegetable market, is a long, low frame house, filled with plain, hard benches, well adapted to a "change of front," for they have no backs to interfere. A real stage is constructed, with foot-lights and curtain, and the flanks display an excellent imitation of private boxes. The orchestra, which, by the way, was the redeeming portion of the entertainment, was made up of amateurs from the various regiments, Ohio furnishing the lion's share. The accomplished leader is a civilian from Ohio, who also excels in the kindred art of photography—the which he pursues in the army for his own advantage, and his customers' accommodation. Order was enforced in last night's entertainment by the presence of a corporal's guard with guns and fixed bayonets. It was a novel entertainment—so completely military. Even the songs, and the "heavy" piece of the evening—"The Rough Diamond"—introduced the soldier and the war in every conceivable manner. The negro came in, of course, on such an occasion. Portions of the performance were encored, and the audience dispersed with a rather favorable feeling toward the efforts of the amateur performers.

Not only do theatrical tendencies give warning of the approach of the gay season, but matrimonial inclinations also confirm the fact. The charms of a Mississippi belle—

a sweet secesher—so entrapped a son of Erin, an artillerist, that he to-day became the happy husband of his lady love. A soldier-parson tied the knot, and was immediately engaged to perform the same kind of service for another military couple this week.

The gayety shadowed forth by the foregoing, is by no means restricted to the white population. The contrabands, of whom there is a large number, are encamped together; of course this throws them into "society" a great deal, and the inevitable result is the growth of the tender passion in the hearts of the young men and maidens there assembled. The chaplain who presides over this dusky encampment, had a call to-day to join the hands of two whose hearts were already one. Finding, however, that there are many under his care, who have been living as man and wife according to the slave custom, but who have never been formally or legally married, he determined to make next Sabbath a grand conjugal day, at which time he proposes to unite in the holy bands of wedlock all those who have heretofore been informally married. It will be *the* wedding day of their recollection.

CHAPTER IV.

WINTER AT CORINTH.

About the middle of December, 1862, Colonel Mersey's Brigade, consisting then of the 81st Ohio, and 12th Illinois Infantry, and Battery I, 1st Mo. light artillery, received marching orders, and moved southward. At this time Gen. Grant was far down in central Mississippi; so far that, with no Union force on the Mobile and Ohio R. R. farther south than Corinth, the rebels had an admirable means in that railroad of throwing troops in his rear, and of effectually cutting his communications. To ascertain if such movement was in progress, and to arrest it if so, General Dodge sent Colonel Mersey's brigade upon this somewhat extended reconnoisance. The troops started with five days rations, but as the country was full of provisions for man and beast, there was no telling from this fact how long the expedition would be gone. No tents were taken, and the troops, especially the recruits of the 81st Ohio had their first experience in marching and bivouacking. The weather was mostly propitious, and the roads in excellent order. Passing through Rienzi, the Brigade deflected a little to the right, and passed through Blackland. At this place, which was reached the second or third day, a few shots were exchanged with a small party of bushwhackers, or straggling soldiers, and a number of them were captured. With this exception, Colonel Mersey met with no opposition. He passed through Guntown and reached Saltillo in a drenching rain. Encamping here, a portion of the command went on to Tupelo, and captured several officers who were too drunk to leave when the place was evacuated by the few troops who had garrisoned it. Finding no enemy, and no appearance of any, and having communicated with a force of cavalry sent from General Grant's main army, Colonel Mersey turned the head of his column homeward, this time taking a road several miles eastward of that on which he had come. Not a shot was exchanged on the return, and the expedition would have been considered fruitless if it had not brought in such large quantities of cotton, mules, horses and contrabands. When at Jacinto, on the return, orders were received from Corinth to hurry to that place. Early the next day the troops were in motion, and so eager were they that by twelve o'clock the brigade marched into Corinth in triumph, their bands playing as blithely, and the men as steady in their step as if returning from the drill-ground. Thus ended what was afterward designated by the regiment as their seven days' march.

Corinth was not found to be quite so desirable a place, on the return of the regiment, as many, while wearied by their marching, had supposed it to be. General Dodge, with almost all the garrison, had gone northward to repel Forrest in his attack on the railroad over which we received our supplies. The great Holly Springs disaster had occurred on the 20th of December, and General Grant was obliged to give up his land approach to Vicksburg and return to Memphis. Forrest, with a very strong mounted force had crossed the Tennessee River, in the vicinity of Clifton, and had made serious attacks on the line of railroad which supplied Corinth. In this condition of affairs, the little garrison at Corinth was suddenly made an outpost, far removed from the main army. Its means of communication being broken, the entire garrison was, on the 22d of December, placed on half rations. This continued for about three weeks, though it occasioned less suffering than many would suppose. Foraging parties were sent out as far as it was safe to venture, and obtained food for the animals as well as limited supplies for the men. One very annoying feature of the position was that the most extravagant rumors of events reached us. A letter written there January 4th, 1863, gives the following account of the bliss of ignorance enjoyed by the troops at that time:

"Up to the present writing, the latest news we have received through the newspapers is to the date of December 17th. But do not think that we have been miserable on account of the failure of the accustomed late papers to reach us. We have had no scarcity of news. Scarcely had communication been destroyed, until we had *reliable* intelligence of a bloody fight in the streets of Jackson, Tennessee, in which our troops were victorious, with a loss of three hundred killed—very few wounded, because cotton bales were used for entrenchments, and nearly all who were shot, were struck in the head. We also had undoubted information of the capture of Richmond. General Banks had sailed up James River, landed, and made a vigorous attack in the rear. This great fact continued to be true for several days, when our attention was drawn to Lee and Burnside. Lee had followed Burnside across the Rappahannock, defeated him, and afterward encountered Sigel, who, aided by Burnside's shattered forces, completely destroyed Lee's whole army. Then came a fresh account of the capture of Richmond. This time it was done by Sigel, who had burned the whole city, and planted the stars and stripes over the ruins. In the meantime we had positive information of the capture of Vicksburg and Mobile. In fact, it required but a moderate stock of credulity to supply any one with more news than the most enterprising editor of a daily paper could furnish. A few incredulous souls, not being able to appreciate the situation, conceived the foolish idea that we were all somewhat in the condition of St. Patrick's snake; and they carried out the simile by asking, day after day, when the mail would come through, and receiving daily the snake's satisfactory assurance—'to-morrow.' But if it had not been for the fact that our supplies were alarmingly short, the most of us would, I suppose, have preferred to have remained isolated from the outer world and all its manifold rumors, knowing that here all the *reliable* news reached us, even in advance of the occurrences themselves."

Notwithstanding this isolated condition and its starvation prospects, the garrison was far from despondent. On Christmas the drill ground south of Corinth was the scene of several races between some of the fine horses owned by officers. On New Years' night a grand military ball was given at the Tishomingo Hotel. The hall was beautifully and tastefully decorated with evergreens and with the battle-stained flags of all the regiments that belonged to the garrison. Corinth, Jackson, Burnsville and Danville were laid under contribution to furnish ladies. A good band was in attendance, and dancing was kept up till the " wee sma' hours."

On the 31st of December, Forrest's great raid culminated in the battle of Parker's Cross Roads, in which he was defeated and driven toward the river. Late in the afternoon of the 1st of January, General Dodge was notified of this, and urged to try to intercept him at Clifton. Orders were immediately issued to the 1st and 2d Brigades, and two batteries of artillery to move. On the 2d the troops started, and at night encamped near Savannah. At midnight a severe rain began, compelling the troops to be all unwilling sentinels. In the morning General Dodge received word that Forrest had crossed. The troops returned to Corinth.

About the 15th of January a small steamer came up the river to Hamburg with supplies, and the hungry troops rejoiced over full rations.

About the 23d of January, 1863, another large steamer arrived at Hamburg with supplies for the garrison at Corinth. It was the steamer J. Raymond, and was convoyed by the little gunboats General Pillow and Alfred Robb. An immense wagon train, escorted by four regiments of infantry and a battery of artillery, was dispatched to bring its cargo, but this not being sufficient, another train of two hundred wagons, escorted by the 27th and

81st Ohio, the 7th and 52d Illinois infantry, and a section of Battery I, 1st Missouri Light Artillery, all under command of Lieut. Col. Adams, 81st Ohio, was sent from Corinth on the morning of the 26th of January. This march and its incidents made it one of the severest hardships which the regiment had yet endured. At three or four o'clock in the afternoon a pitiless storm of rain began to fall. The ground was already muddy, and this rain only served to make the mud thinner and deeper. With two regiments of troops and two hundred wagons to precede the 81st, the condition of that clayey road can be imagined but not described. Mercilessly came the rain until dark, and then the 81st was still two miles from Hamburg. Here the road runs through a wide swamp, which, during the previous summer, had been spanned by a corduroy road for the use of the army. It was now covered with mud of various depths, and the men, drenched with the rain, and unable to distinguish the treacherous pitfalls from the solid ground, plunged straight through like so many hogs. Every few feet some luckless fellow would go sprawling hopelessly down into the mud covering himself all over with the Tennessee soil. All the while it continued raining, and there were cheerless forebodings of a comfortless night, when the soldiers contemplated their wet and muddy clothing, the unbounded mud and the extreme scarcity of rails in the vicinity of Hamburg. Usually the soldier cares little for wet clothing during the day if he has a prospect of being able to enjoy a bright fire at night. That night, on arriving at Hamburg, instead of bivouacking on shore, where by blazing fires the discomforts of the day's march would soon have been forgotten, the 81st was ordered aboard a barge. Any one who has traveled with troops on our steamers can imagine how much of comfort there was in that condition. Think of a tired soldier having walked twenty miles through mud and rain, until his clothing is entirely saturated with water, and then, with his chilling garments clinging closely to his shivering, hungering body, he is deposited like so much freight, in the damp hold of a filthy barge, where not so much as the smell of fire could reach him, and where there was no possible opportunity to obtain a cup of the soldier's *sine qua non*—hot coffee. This was the hard lot of the 81st Ohio that night. A few bales of hay were issued to the soldiers which they scattered over the damp floor for beds. On it, wet, muddy and cold, they threw themselves down supperless to sleep. Here and there some luckless one who could not find where to lay his head, could be heard all through the night shivering with cold.

When morning dawned, it was discovered by the regiment that this merciless exposure had not been without an object. It was found that other troops had also embarked on the Raymond, and that a departure before morning had been contemplated. It was for a no less pretentious object than the surprise and capture of the forces under Roddy, who was encamped near Florence, Alabama, with about 4,000 rebel cavalry. The two little gunboats were to accompany for the purpose of silencing batteries on shore, shelling the woods and covering the landing of troops. Then "by a combined attack by the land and naval forces" the cavalry were to be taken by storm and the expedition to return in triumph. It was doubtless a brilliant plan, and it was not the fault of the commander, Col. Rice, that it failed. Daylight found the J. Raymond, which in the "piping times of peace" towed Dan Rice's great show from city to city, now towing another Rice's menagerie up the Tennessee. The gunboats advanced bravely. All went gloriously until at a distance of three miles from Hamburg, the J. Raymond sounded a halt, and put ashore to tie up. It was soon discovered that one of her wheels had been run on the bottom when starting, until its axle was lifted out of its place, bursting off the cap, which, with the brass boxing had fallen into the river. It was surmised by some that the accident was not purely accidental, as the officers of the boat were averse to risking their lives and property in a fight. A council of war was held, composed of representatives from the army and the navy, which soon decided to return to Hamburg, and give up the expedition. The return was made on one wheel by the J. Raymond, and the troops disembarked. After waiting an hour to cook the first meal since leaving Corinth, the 81st took up their homeward march, and notwithstanding the state of the roads, they reached their camp, twenty miles in seven hours.

The month of March, 1863 was spent in garrison without particular incident. The spring brought with it the old desire for renovation—and soldiers, obedient to the law which has governed their mothers from time immemorial, proceeded to clear away the *debris* which had accumulated during the winter, and to make a thorough remodeling of their camps. The 81st Ohio rescued its camp from the disorder in which it stood all winter, and gave it the charm of regularity. When all was set in order a train of wagons was sent to the pine regions, only a few miles distant, to obtain young pines with which to decorate the camp. It required but a day to obtain the trees and plant them; and what an effect! The bare white tents were relieved by the grateful green of the pines, and the soldiers were in ecstacies on beholding the wonderful change. It was found that it paid even for soldiers to give some attention to the amenities of life.

On the 7th of April, the 81st celebrated the anniversary of the battle of Shiloh. On very short notice, a very good substantial supper for every man in the regiment was spread in camp; and just when the regiment returned, wearied and hungry, from the afternoon review, the men were called to the tables and bountifully supplied with the good things thereon. It was intended to have had a dance in the open air at night, but it was found impossible to obtain material for bonfires, and the dance had to be abandoned. As it was, however, the supper put the regiment in the best possible humor, and all retired glad that they were at Shiloh a year ago, and that they were here now.

CHAPTER V.

EXPEDITION TO TUSCUMBIA.

On the 15th of April, 1863, Gen. Dodge moved from Corinth with almost his entire force. The previous day an attack had been made upon the outpost of Glendale, and this seemed to the rebels as the occasion of General Dodge's movement, though in reality quite a different object was in view. The cavalry chased the rebels away from Glendale, and the infantry moved on leisurely afterward, encamping the first night at Burnsville. The next day the march was continued a few miles beyond Iuka to a point a mile or two from Bear Creek, which was said to be defended by the rebel cavalry under Roddy. On the 17th Gen. Dodge moved with the intention of crossing the stream. It was almost too deep to ford and there was no bridge; the opposite bank was favorable for defense. placing a section of artillery in position, and shelling the ford a little while, General Dodge compelled the rebels, who had no artillery, to flee, and our cavalry, finding a shallow place, crossed and pursued. The infantry was immediately ordered to cross also. How was it to be done? The water was not only deep but swift. To attempt to wade would be but to be carried away by the current. To provide against this, a rope was stretched from shore to shore just above the water, which served to steady the steps of the soldiers. It was rare sport for most of them. The day was mild, and the water felt cool and refreshing. Doffing their clothes and swinging them with knapsack, haversack and cartridge box across their guns, which they carried on their shoulders, in order to keep their powder dry, the soldiers, with songs and cheers and exclamations of delight, marched single file across the angry stream. It was to all a novel way of crossing a stream. The whole division went into bivouac on crossing, but the cavalry, which, under the impetuous Col. Cornyn, had pressed on farther than was expected, met with a considerable force of the enemy and sent back for help. Col. Bane's brigade was instantly ordered forward, and came very near entrapping the rebel force.

But as the object of the expedition was to co-operate with Col. Straight's command, which was coming from Nashville, Gen. Dodge collected his troops again at Bear Creek and waited for the arrival of Col. Straight. This command having reached Eastport on the river, disembarked and marched to Bear Creek. The plan was for Gen. Dodge to move with his force to Tuscumbia, Col. Straight accompanying. There, while Gen. Dodge manœuvered to distract the attention of the rebels, Col. Straight was to move rapidly to the south and east, and do the work of destruction assigned him in Georgia. As this movement was one of some historical interest, and as it was at that time the most extended march and campaign the regiment had made. I propose to extract freely from accounts written at the time.

"On the morning of the 23d of April, at an early hour, the whole column was put in motion on the road toward Tuscumbia. The rain had put the roads in the finest condition, and the rested troops marched gaily along in the happiest humor, glad to see so much beauty as the green hills on either side of the road afforded. Beginning a few miles east of Bear Creek, there is a large upland valley, remarkable for its direction, being at right angles with the streams. Along this valley runs the Memphis and Charleston railroad and the wagon road to Tuscumbia.

On either side of the road, at various distances, are the finest of green-topped hills, with just enough irregularity to relieve them of monotony. They bear a striking resemblance to the graceful hills along the Miami and Scioto rivers in Ohio, except that just now they are mottled with the dark green of the pines which are scattered among the oaks and other trees of lighter colored foliage.

About 3 P. M. the column had crossed Cane Creek and gone into camp, the left resting almost on the Tennessee river. The cavalry was carefully secreted along the base of the hills on the right, while the infantry was boldly placed in the open fields. Scarcely had the men time to prepare supper until orders came to fall in and advance. On the right of the railroad Gen. Sweeney advanced with a regiment or two and some artillery, while on the left, Col. Morton advanced his brigade, with artillery accompanying.

The Eighty-first Ohio, with Company C and a platoon of Company I, as skirmishers, was in advance and made a splendid appearance as its long lines extended across the open fields. Very soon the rebel position was discovered, and with the impression that they were supplied with artillery, Gen. Sweeney sent in a few shells, but without eliciting any reply. Then Col. Morton sent from his guns a few of the same kind of messengers with same result. It was obvious that the rebels were only holding the place with a small force, yet it was desirable to drive them away, lest during the night they should strengthen the position. The whole line advanced. It looked hazardous. Our forces were in open ground, descending to a small stream, while on the opposite side was "Rock Cut," a narrow gap where the railroad passes between two sentinel hills, and where a small force could easily have wrought great damage to us. But still the lines advanced, the little stream was crossed, the opposite heights gained and the gap secured, the rebels incontinently fleeing before us. A portion of General Sweeney's troops pushed on to Little Bear Creek, on the opposite bank of which the rebels were strongly posted. The Eighty-first Ohio bivouacked at the eastern end of "Rock Cut" for the night. Before daylight of the 24th the troops of Gen. Sweeney, including the 81st Ohio, temporarily acting under his orders, were silently placed in new positions, it having been supposed that the rebels were about to attack us at daylight. But in this we were disappointed. A little while before sunrise, Company C of the Eighty-first Ohio and Company B of the Second Iowa, were deployed as skirmishers, and ordered forward until within sight of Little Bear Creek. Without opposition the long line penetrated the thick woods in its front and moved on unsupported, a mile at least, when, coming to the edge of a narrow field, it halted in full sight of the disputed stream. The rebels on the opposite shore immediately took to horse and galloped off. A few men from the skirmish line went down to the creek and reported no enemy there, but as the crest of the hill above was sufficient for the masking of any amount of hostile forces, it was deemed prudent to push the reconnoisance farther. This was done, and the rebels were found flying. Gen. Dodge, with a small cavalry force, immediately passed over the crest of the hill and in a few minutes made the entry into Tuscumbia. Immediately the whole column was in motion, and so prompt was the movement that the rear of our column had reached the heights overlooking the town before the rebels were entirely gone. Capts. Spencer and Carpenter of Gen. Dodge's staff pressed too closely on the rebel rearguard and were sharply fired on.

Tuscumbia is one of the oldest towns in the State, and is remarkable for its beauty of situation and its wonderful springs. Okocopasaw, as the native Indian spoke it when he meant cold water, is the name of the largest spring, which gushes out from beneath an overhanging rock, at a rate of four miles an hour, and with a volume sufficient to form a stream three feet deep and from fifteen to thirty feet wide. A rude stone wall has been built on either side of the basin, just below where the water comes out, and a stone stairway leads down to the surface of the water. "Aunt Susey's Spring" is another smaller one, farther to the west. Several other smaller and nameless ones are found along the base of the little bank on which Tuscumbia is situated. The stream formed by these springs is sufficient to supply motive power for several mills.

The town itself, in its buildings, is ordinary; but the shrubbery and flowers, of which there is the richest profusion, render it a paradise even in its desolation. War has paralysed its business; but nature, in defiance of armies, has made Tuscumbia charming. Our soldiers, who have for a year seen only the dull desolation of Corinth, are delighted with the view of civilization and refinement which is given them here."

Col. Cornyn with the cavalry pushed on after the flying rebels, and overtaking them near Leighton, ten miles east of Tuscumbia, had a sharp fight, driving them in three hours a distance of as many miles.

Gen. Dodge remained at Tuscumbia on the 25th and 26th, using every effort to complete the equipment of Col. Straight's command for the important expedition it was about to undertake. He even gave up one-third of the animals belonging to his own command, (except cavalry,) and yet there was not enough. Col. Straight was obliged to spend the first day or two of his march in pressing animals to mount the remainder of his men. It is perhaps owing to this that his expedition was not more successful. However, at midnight of the 26th he started, Gen. Dodge having thoroughly occupied the rebel cavalry so as to divert attention from Col. Straight's movements. In order still to keep the enemy deceived, Gen. Dodge moved early on the morning of the 27th with his whole force eastwardly.

Leaving Tuscumbia, the country becomes more like an elevated plateau, flanked on each side with a low and tolerably regular range of hills. Large plantations, elegantly adorned by the true Southern mansions, and dotted with the neat little villages of negro quarters, now all vacant, are to be seen all along the road. For a distance of several miles no stream is in view, but numerous ponds and sink holes are everywhere to be found.

Gen. Sweeney, with his brigade in the advance, found no interruption until after he had passed the little village of Leighton several miles, and reached the stream known as Town Creek. Here, on the eastern side he found a force of cavalry and artillery. Arriving nearly at night, he only threw a few shells across, and then the troops went into camp for the night.

On the 28th of April occurred what, by a little license

may be termed the battle of Town Creek. Quite early in the morning we were aroused by a sharp fire of musketry between our pickets and those of the enemy, posted on opposite sides of the stream. Not long after daylight our troops were under arms, and having two or three batteries in position we commenced a deliberate cannonading of the enemy's position. Roddy had but a few guns, and they being of an inferior range, he soon discovered that they were no match for Capts. Welker and Richardson, and ceased firing. Capt. Tannrath, with his battery devoted his attention to clearing the woods of sharp shooters on the left of the railroad, where they had been of considerable annoyance. His accurately thrown shells soon drove them to the high ground beyond range.

About ten o'clock the enemy suddenly opened with artillery on one of our batteries near a brick house, with such excellent range that the first shot struck in the building. Anxious for an opportunity to give them a taste of our shell, an immediate response by two or three of our batteries was made, though the rebel position was so well chosen that it was almost impossible to dislodge them. The rebels continued to throw shell and solid shot, the latter flying far to the rear of our batteries, while the former burst long before they reached our guns. Company B, of the 81st Ohio, being deployed as skirmishers along the bank to guard against attempts at crossing, was somewhat annoyed by these premature explosions. The only casualty, however, was a pretty severe flesh wound received by Private Arthur Hall, who was struck below the left shoulder by a piece of shell. In about an hour the rebel guns ceased and ours fired but very slowly.

Preparations were now made for crossing the stream. It was a deep, narrow stream, with precipitous banks, and swollen by the rain of the previous night, it was entirely too deep and swift to be forded by either cavalry or artillery, and the only bridge was the one at the railroad. Placing Captain Tannrath's battery in a position to command the bridge, General Dodge, who had been on the ground all the morning, ordered Colonel Morton to send a regiment from his brigade across the bridge to cover the crossing of such forces as should be ordered to follow. The Colonel chose to send the 81st Ohio, and Lieutenant-Colonel Adams commanding, ordered Company F to cross the bridge and deploy to the right of the railroad. The bridge being partially hidden by trees, this movement was promptly executed without opposition, and a few minutes afterward the whole regiment, accompanied by General Dodge on foot, crossed the bridge, and deploying Company C as skirmishers on the left of the railroad, formed close to the creek. No sooner had the regiment crossed than the Pioneer corps began tearing down some buildings on the west side of the stream, and using the lumber in flooring the bridge to facilitate the crossing. When this was done, Lieutenant-Colonel Phillips, with four companies of the 9th Illinois, crossed, and deploying as skirmishers formed on the extreme left. Then, taking command of the whole line of skirmishers, he began an advance. Several rebels had been seen already up the railroad, and a squad had been fired at while reconnoitering our line on the left of the railroad. So soon as Colonel Phillips emerged from the woods which skirted the bank of the creek, he saw before him a vast open plantation rising gently some five or six hundred yards to what seemed a ridge.

On the ridge was a dwelling house, a cotton house and a little village of negro huts, near which the rebel artillery had been posted in the morning. Seeing no hiding place for the rebels except toward the left where there was a woods, Col. Phillips determined to halt the skirmishers on the right of the railroad, and swing around the right of the remaining line toward the supposed

5

hiding place. In doing so, the right soon reached the top of the ridge and found numerous squads of rebels on horseback, hovering around, just behind the crest of the ridge, or rather the summit of the elevated plateau, some of them almost directly in rear of the right of our line. As soon as this was discovered, Col. Phillips halted the line, and sent four men from Company C, 81st Ohio, from the right of the line to a little eminence on the right to wake up whoever might be behind it. They advanced steadily to the fence, and looking over they perceived several horsemen within range. They fired, and one of the horsemen was dismounted. The others moved off, and our four men started boldly in pursuit. But like the bonnets and plaids of the warriors of Rhoderic Dhu, the butternut hats and coats began to appear from every fence corner, and from behind every bush, until quite a considerable force was developed. Still the four men kept on, going straight toward the whole lot, until they were ordered to come back, which they did with great reluctance.

General Dodge had remained all this while with the 81st Ohio, watching the movement, and superintending the crossing of other troops on the right. It was now about 4 P. M., and by this time portions of General Sweeney's and Colonel Bane's brigades had effected a crossing farther to the right. The General determined to make a thorough reconnoisance of the whole space in front, and, if possible, give the enemy battle. For this purpose he ordered out a grand line of skirmishers. Taking the railroad for the center, he deployed to the right and left one of the longest lines of skirmishers which we had then seen. Five companies (all large) of the 81st Ohio were out: F, I and C deployed, and D and K following close in reserve. A like number from at least three other regiments made a line which was estimated to be two miles in length. The ground was almost wholly clear, and descending, with but slight irregularities, it was possible from various points to obtain a view of the whole line, with its dark little bodies of companies in reserve following close after it at regular intervals, while at a little greater distance to the rear could be seen the main reserves moving in splendid order, with their flashing banners unfurled, and floating majestically in the brightening rays of the declining sun. It was a sight to move one's soul; and what gave it additional interest was, that all along our whole front, at a distance just out of range of our guns, the rebel horsemen kept slowly moving on, no doubt enamored of the splendid spectacle presented to their view. Now and then some lingerer would find himself saluted by the music of our balls, and would hasten forward, out of range. Still, steadily the grand line, with its primary and secondary reserves, moved on, halting occasionally to correct the alignment or to make observations. As steadily, halting when we did, the rebels moved, taking care to not stop within range. Once on the left, a bold rebel remained secreted within a little skirt of woods until we came in good range, when he fired, the ball touching the fingers of Sergeant Workman, Company I, 81st Ohio, inflicting only a slight wound. Quick as a flash a dozen of our Enfields answered his lone shot, and he was not bold enough to try another.

In this manner we proceeded until sunset, when the line had advanced three miles from the creek, and both flanks had reached a dense forest, while the center was but a short distance from the edge of the clear ground. So far we had moved without opposition; the rebels slowly retiring before us without evincing any desire to accept battle. At dusk the line was halted, and soon after was silently withdrawn to the opposite side of Town Creek. The object of the expedition had been as fully accomplished as it was possible to do. General Dodge had kept the enemy engaged for two days and nights, during which time it was hoped Colonel Straight would be far on his way. The sequel proved that that officer was delayed for the purpose of obtaining stock to mount his troops until the first day was virtually wasted. The next day about noon his movement was communicated to the force before General Dodge, and it was withdrawn as quickly as possible thereafter.

General Dodge therefore returned to Corinth as expeditiously as possible, burning all corn and supplies of every kind that could be found.

The march was the most extended the regiment had then taken, being one of eighteen days duration, yet it was the best. Excellent discipline rendered it at once the most pleasant and the most orderly movement they had yet made, and although the rations were short at the close of the campaign, and the troops weary with the march, yet on the 2d of May the regiment marched into camp with banners flying, music sounding, and step as regular as if returning from drill, *with every man in his place.*

Immediately upon the return from this expedition, the 81st Ohio completed their very comfortable summer quarters of little wooden structures covered and enclosed by clap-boards made by the soldiers. The work was scarcely finished until orders were received to change camp to a position about a mile south of Corinth, lately occupied by the Ohio Brigade. This change was less unwelcome to the 81st, from the fact that it was assigned to the excellent quarters constructed by the 27th Ohio. This position had also the additional advantage of being in a beautiful grove, affording a most welcome shade in the hot days. Water was abundant and near at hand, an excellent drill ground was contiguous to the camp, and there was nothing wanting to complete the pleasantness of the situation.

CHAPTER VI.

POCAHONTAS AND PULASKI.

But the soldier never can be sure of the continuance of any "good thing" in his military life. The change in the line of communication from that by way of Columbus, Kentucky, to the direct line from Memphis, made about this time, and the consequent changing of garrison, made it necessary for General Dodge to distribute a portion of the garrison of Corinth along the road toward Memphis. The Second Brigade was ordered to Pocahontas, about twenty miles from Corinth. On the 3d of June, the 81st Ohio very reluctantly started from their beautiful encampment. Not leaving Corinth until nearly noon, the regiment had not gone half the distance until a terrific storm of wind and rain came upon them, completely drenching every man, and rendering the roads almost impassable. The same storm blew down a number of trees in the encampment which the regiment had just left, crushing a number of the houses in such a manner that if the regiment had been there death must have ensued. As it was, although no one was killed, yet all passed a most disagreeable night in bivouac—a condition not at all ameliorated by the remembrance of the almost princely quarters they had occupied the previous night. About noon on the 4th, the Second Brigade reached Pocahontas. It was anything but a pleasant prospect. An old, dilapidated village, whose very slatternliness was sufficient to make one melancholy, answered to the name of Pocahontas. It had one redeeming feature: it had never yet been occupied permanently by either Federal or Confederate forces, and was consequently in that pure state of nature which is so desirable for an encampment. The 81st Ohio was assigned to a tolerably pleasant position in the edge of a woods near the town, and this time, disdaining to build permanent quarters from which they could at any moment be ousted without their consent, they pitched their tents in true military style. One or two of the companies, however, having faith in the permanency of their location, erected temporary wooden quarters. Captain Henry's company (H) was ordered to Muddy Creek, about two miles west of Pocahontas, for the purpose of guarding the railroad bridge over that stream.

By degrees the position at Pocahontas became more inviting. The bustle occasioned by such a body of troops infused some life into the dull town. The country in the vicinity was productive, and the troops had their tables bountifully supplied with all the fruits and vegetables which the market afforded. The duty was chiefly formal picket duty—no drills being had on account of the hot weather. In this easy way the summer was passed, without any incidents of importance.

It was in July of this year that General Oglesby, who had been made Major-General for his gallant action at the battle of Corinth, and who, for some time had been in command of the Left Wing, 16th Army Corps, was compelled to resign. As his parting order makes honorable mention of the Second Brigade, and of the 81st Ohio, I am sure every member of the regiment will be glad to preserve, in this form, those words of their gallant commander. It will be observed that, with characteristic modesty, he makes no allusion to the fact that his wound, received at Corinth, was the sole cause of the physical infirmity which compelled him to resign.

"HEADQUARTERS LEFT WING 16TH ARMY CORPS,
MEMPHIS, TENNESSEE, July 6, 1863.

'General Orders, No. 21 :

"Continued pain, resulting from physical infirmity, assures me that I am not able faithfully to discharge the duties of the high position given me by the President of the United States.

"I have therefore tendered my resignation as a Major-General of United States Volunteers. In taking leave of a command, with a portion of which I have been so long and so intimately associated, I may be excused for indulging in the expression of feelings which have grown into sentiments of the most ardent attachment.

"It will be remembered by them also that I have never officially reported the part taken by the Second Brigade of the Second Division of the Army of the Tennessee, in the terrible battle fought on the 3d day of October, A. D. 1862, at Corinth. Now, for them, let me do something like justice to the devoted courage of the 9th, 12th and 66th Illinois, and 22d and 81st Ohio Volunteers, and to Mersey, Chetlain, Burke, Wood and Morton, their able and worthy commanders; to Colonel Mersey, as the command of the Brigade fell upon him when I left the field.

It must be recorded of those soldiers, that no men ever fought more daringly, when in the final charge on Friday afternoon. They actually drove three times their number of stubborn men fairly from the field, and from the high road to Corinth, then not one-half mile distant.

"I shall always believe that nothing but the desperate fighting of the Second Division of the Army of the Tennessee, on the main Chewalla Road, saved Corinth from the possession of the enemy on Friday afternoon, for which I shall never cease to thank you. Fellow-soldiers, I part with you with much regret. I have known your sufferings, and with pride have witnessed your devotion to our common and noble cause. You have endured one hardship, to encounter another; have gone from one field of victory to another of blood, and have at all times felt and so acted as to satisfy good men that you had honor and a country at stake, and have hesitated at no risk to save either. Your country must love you. Your country does love you. The world in all time to come will honor you. Reverence for you must be eternal. The obscure soldier, who toils through this war, will have an unwritten but an unforgotten history, an ever present conscience repaying him with its rich rewards.

"Faithful soldier, thou hast served thy country well. I shall never forget you, nor shall I abate my efforts to sustain you at home. That man in the loyal States, who is not thought and soul for you, for the Union, and for the war, is no friend of mine, is no true friend of humanity anywhere. I reflect with just pride upon the names of those gallant officers who have led you to battle, sometimes under my command. How much the country owes them; how much they are to be honored; the discreet and indefatigable Dodge, Sweeney, Mersey, Bane, Rice, Mizner, M'Crillis, Hatch, Cornyn and Phillips. Amongst those of former days, I well remember Logan, M'Arthur, Ransom, Lawler, the lamented Wallace, and others equally worthy. With such men to lead and inspire you we cannot fail. The proud army of the Great West, with scarcely a reverse, presents to the nation a boquet of victory, the gratitude and admiration of the whole people.

"You may well say: This war can not last much longer. You, who have witnessed traitors with haughty pretension crouch at your feet for mercy; the mansions of the domineering rich turned into boarding houses, and the chivalry turned landlord and lady, for the entertainment of Yankee officers. Those who have spurned, beg for favors at your hands; and swearing a new allegiance for protection to property, meanly violate it to serve a rebel. It is fit and proper that such a people, who foolishly wage such a war, should at last meet face to face the black race of the South, bend to the rod of the slaves they have so long outraged, and tremble before the men proclaimed by them to have no rights. A just retribution, one they can not avoid; the humiliation their own bold treason has brought upon them; a resort that needs no justification in the sight of God or man, for it is right.

[Signed]   R. J. OGLESBY,
                                   Major-General."

So highly was General Oglesby esteemed, that instead of accepting his resignation, he was granted six months' leave of absence.

During the stay of the regiment at Pocahontas, the most of the watching for the enemy, and almost all the marches against him, were made by the mounted force—the 9th Illinois, under command of the dashing and gallant Lieut. Col. Phillips. It is true that in September, when Forrest made serious attacks upon the railroad at Collierville, where a part of the division, to which the 81st belonged, had quite a severe fight, a part of the regiment was moved up to Grand Junction, but it was but a temporary absence.

In October a good position was selected, and in prospect of spending the winter there, the troops went to work with a will to construct winter quarters. The finest splitting timber was selected, and great care was exercised in making the boards. Each company had its ground accurately staked off—the streets between the companies were of uniform width, and the quarters were ordered to be built with the same regard for regularity. Busy hands plied earnestly day after day, until the camp was completed, and the regiment was in ecstacies over the beautiful and comfortable quarters erected. Visions of cheerful winter evenings before their bright, old-fashioned fires, and thoughts of comfort upon returning from some cheerless tour of picket or fatigue duty, filled their imaginations, and they felt as if they hardly needed the sympathy so often tendered by friends at home for the poor soldier. But, alas!

> "The best laid plans o' *mice* and *men*
> Gang aft aglee,
> And bring us nought but grief an' pain
> For promised joy."

A fatality seemed to attend the efforts of the 81st in the matter of providing comfortable quarters. They had left a fine camp at Corinth, after enjoying it but about three weeks, and now Camp Brough—a name given to this encampment in honor of the election of Gov. Brough, the news of which reached them about the time the work was done—even Camp Brough had to be evacuated. General

Sherman was passing that way on his famous march from Memphis, and, as if catching the infection of his wonderful energy, all the troops of the Left Wing, 16th Army Corps, now commanded by General Dodge, prepared to move in the same direction. The 81st Ohio left Pocahontas about the last of October, expecting to accompany Sherman and join the army about Chattanooga.

Passing through Corinth, Iuka and Eastport, the 81st crossed the Tennessee at the latter point and moved on through Tennessee. The roads were generally in excellent condition, the weather mild and favorable, great care was taken in regulating the distance marched each day, and in selecting places of encampment, and the result was that the march was but a pleasure trip. No lagging behind, no straggling, but a continuous care for the comfort, on the part of officers, and a respect for orders on the part of the men. At one time, after crossing the Tennessee, a portion of the wagon train was attacked by a small party of guerrillas, and two wagons captured and burnt, the mules being taken away. The party was immediately driven off, and no more interruptions occurred. The troops found an abundance of sweet potatoes, chickens, turkeys, hogs and cattle with which to eke out very palatably the scanty rations with which they left the river. The principle of subsisting on the enemy had already been sufficiently approved and applied by this command to enable the soldiers to unearth potatoes or catch a chicken with very little compunction of conscience. However, this matter was generally done in a lawful manner. Foraging details were made, to obtain whatever was necessary for the command.

On the 10th of November, General Dodge's command reached Pulaski, the county seat of Giles county, Tenn. Here, very unexpectedly to himself and to his troops, he received orders to halt, and to garrison and rebuild the

Tennessee and Alabama Railroad, running from Nashville to Decatur. This was, in effect, an order to go into winter quarters, but as it was not immediately communicated to the troops, and remembering their former experience, the 81st Ohio boys were slow to attempt building huts. Upon leaving Pocahontas all tents, except three or four had been stored at Corinth, and the troops were thus left shelterless in the beginning of winter. To add to this discomfort of the situation, the place selected for the camp of the 81st was on a rather steep hill-side, in an open field, on a soil which, during a rain, formed first-class mud. On that bleak hill-side the troops tried in vain to find comfort, by building little rail pens and covering them with their water-proof blankets. It is not wonderful that the loose plank lying about Pulaski found its way, during the nights, to these miserable excuses for tents; nor is it at all wonderful that this tendency toward camp, exhibited by loose plank, ended there. It was currently reported, in the language of one of the soldiers, who had witnessed the phenomenon, "that if a soldier only leaned against a board fence in the night, the nails would drop out, and the boards would stick to his clothes until he reached camp!"

Be this as it may, it is certain that in a short time there was such a collection of odds and ends of boards in camp, that a moderate degree of comfort was obtained, although the structures put up were of all conceivable shapes and sizes. Messengers were dispatched to Corinth to bring on the tents, but having to come by water to Nashville, they were a long time delayed. When they arrived, the tents were used as roofing to comfortable and moderately uniform houses.

Company A was soon detached and sent to Wales, a station on the railroad, about four miles from Pulaski, where it remained all winter. Companies B, E, F, G and K, under command of Major Evans, were sent to Sam's

Mills, about six miles north-east of Pulaski. In a short time Major Evans, with companies B, E and F, was ordered to Nance's Mills, near Cornersville, leaving Captain Overmyer in command of the two companies at Sam's Mills. Headquarters of the regiment remained at Pulaski, with the four companies left there.

The object of holding these mills was to enable the command to eat up the garnered grain of that hitherto well-filled depot of supplies for the rebels. It was well known that the large surplus quantities of wheat and corn, if not used by our forces, would, in some way, either fall into the hands of the rebels, or form a very tempting bait to a starved command to make a raid. So the very fine steam mills above mentioned were appropriated to Union millers in blue, and were used to their utmost capacity in grinding flour to supply the troops of General Dodge's command. The citizens were encouraged to bring in their wheat to the mills, and voluntarily turn it over to the military authorities, in which case they received for it a fair market price in vouchers that were paid immediately. But if they refused to bring forward their produce, then it was seized by the troops, and vouchers given which could only be paid upon proof of loyalty.

The plan worked admirably. The farmers gladly availed themselves of so good a market, and the mills were kept running day and night. Under the superintendence of Captain W. H. Hill, 81st Ohio, who was detailed as Superintendent of all the mills, the garrison at Pulaski was kept constantly supplied with flour and meal, so that, except for the mounted command, no hard bread at all was issued to the troops. The same regulations were made in reference to hogs and cattle, and of these, too, the troops had an abundance.

CHAPTER VII.

AT PULASKI.

Major Evans had a few of his men mounted, and spent a good portion of time in scouring the country in pursuit of a gang of guerrillas that infested that vicinity. On one of these occasions, one of his party, little Johnny Nott, as he was called, a member of Company E, 81st Ohio, performed a gallant action, which deserves to be remembered.

Young Nott, being somewhat in advance of the rest, observed a Confederate Captain on horseback a short distance before him. Immediately Johnny put spurs to his horse, and started toward the Captain, who esteeming discretion to be the better part of valor, attempted to escape by flight. Fortunately Nott's horse was a very fine one, while the Confederate charger was not good in a retreat. Each moment carried the two desperate riders farther away from the Major's force, while it also lessened the distance between themselves. Faster and faster flew the Federal soldier; nearer and nearer he approached the flying "chivalry." When the rebel was within hailing distance, Johnny, to his horror, discovered him attempting to draw a revolver from a scabbard at his back. Young Nott called to him to halt, but still he kept on, busy in trying to extricate his revolver. Knowing that time was everything in this condition of affairs, Johnny boldly dashed alongside the rebel, and pointing a revolver at his face, a second time ordered him to halt. The Captain halted. Being unable still to draw his stubborn revolver, he had no choice but to surrender to this mere boy, and Johnny brought him back in triumph to the remainder of the party, who were thus first informed of the adventure. The officer was Captain Lewis, of the 53d Tennessee, and was just going back to his regiment, after enjoying a short furlough at home in that vicinity.

In acknowledgement of his gallantry in this affair, little Johnny Nott was permitted to retain the revolver which he captured.

The winter was passed by the regiment in much the same routine. The portion stationed at the mills worked at preparing and hauling saw logs, and at confiscating such forage as they needed in addition to what the citizens voluntarily brought in and turned over. Those stationed at Pulaski had regular and frequent duty at picket, forage and fatigue duty. As a picture of the usual experience at that time, I extract from a letter written January 9, 1864:

"The old year died in a storm of wind and snow and hail. Hoary winter, with his beard of icicles, and his breath of frost, triumphantly ushered in the new year, and placed him on his icy throne. Every wind and zephyr caught the spirit of the new dynasty, and straightway, like couriers, they sped over the land, carrying with them the chill that encircled the throne. High carnival for Winter! A new year inaugurated under his auspices. Right vigorously does he use his power. Perhaps, as around our northern homes the wintry blasts howl, and the snow flies in eddying whirls, and the air becomes like a knife, while within-doors the grates glow with warmth-giving coals, and the cabin hearths are ablaze with the roaring, crackling winter fires—perhaps in our homes there are hearts that shudder as they think of some loved one in their circle, now absent in the army, and wonder if he is not cold and shivering on a cheerless picket post. 'Oh, where is my boy to-night?' is the anxious inquiry of many a mother's heart, as she looks out on the wintry scene.

"Alas! that I can not say that the soldiers do not suffer! Winter brings no cessation of duty. As many men stand as sentinels around this command when the thermometer falls below zero as when the sun sends down his kindliest rays. The Quartermasters send as many wagons over the frozen ground for forage and supplies as they sent when the ground was smooth. The teamsters and train guards are not lessened in number. Yet, after all, there is more solicitude for our comfort in the homes we have left, than we feel here. Each soldier makes it his special duty to provide for his own comfort, and the result is that he suffers comparatively little, and complains less than if he depended upon others. If on picket, he passes his two hours of duty as best he may, knowing that at the end of his 'trick' he has four hours at his own disposal, in which time he can provide a fire. He does not sit down helplessly, and whine because the Government does not provide him a warm shelter—he builds one for himself, and if on returning to the same post to duty, he finds his shelter burned, he sheds no childish tears over his misfortune, but with a patience and cheerfulness that would do honor to the traditional spider, with a broken web, he builds again and again for the hundredth time.

"The citizens of this vicinity say that not since 1837, has there been such cold weather as that of the past week. Yet, notwithstanding the number of men exposed, there has been no case of severe freezing among them all. Here and there an ear or a finger has been 'frosted,' but there have been no serious cases."

During the months of December and January, the regiment was intensely excited on the subject of re-enlisting, under the provisions of the order from the War Department for the organization of a veteran force. By this order troops who had less than a year to serve under their existing enlistment, and who had served at least two years, could, by re-enlisting for three years or during the war, unless sooner discharged, obtain a discharge from their present enlistment, get the bounty of one hundred dollars which was to be paid at the end of their three years' service, have a furlough of thirty days immediately upon re-enlisting, and get a veteran bounty in instalments amounting in all to $402.

Five companies of the regiment, B, C, D, E and F came clearly under the provisions of the order, but the remaining five had only been in service since October, 1862, and had consequently, not fulfilled one of the requirements—that of having already served two years. But they claimed that they had less than a year to serve, as they insisted that they had been enlisted for the unexpired term of the regiment, which would make their term of service expire in the autumn of 1864. Unfortunately their muster-in rolls were all made in the usual form, declaring that " the men and officers above named were accepted into the service of the United States for the term of three years, unless sooner discharged, from this date." And, although the mustering officer, in explanation at the time of the muster-in, stated distinctly that these were only necessary formal words, and he would muster them in for three years, with the understanding that one year had already expired, yet on application to the War Department in the matter, Secretary Stanton peremptorily decided that the muster-in rolls should, in all cases, determine the date of muster-out. Pending this application, an effort was made among the men of these companies to ascertain how many of them would re-enlist as veterans, in case they would be allowed to do so, and fully three-fourths of them were found willing to re-enlist. Of course, the decision above referred to deprived them of the privilege, and restricted the enlistment of veterans to the five old companies.

There were many reasons why it was not extremely popular in the regiment to re-enlist. It required the re-enlistment of at least three-fourths of the number of men present in a company or regiment to enable it to go home as an organization, and retain the same organization. The cutting off of the five new companies made it impossible for the regiment to go home together, and hence effort had to be left to the companies. Here various reasons operated to deter the men. Fears of being transferred to some strange company, or regiment, deterred some; the thought that if they re-enlisted they would only make the draft, which was then impending, more easy on some cowardly copperhead, who needed a schooling in the ranks, had its influence on many. Others received letters from home begging them not to re-enter the service—saying that three years of faithful service was enough for those who went at the first call, without hope of reward, especially when the North was full of able-bodied men who had never been in the service at all.

Notwithstanding all these disadvantages, I am proud to be able to say that in this regiment, at least, patriotism triumphed over self-interest, and such reasons as these influenced those who could not have been induced by the reward in a furlough and the bounty. Said one—"I will re-enlist because I know the Government needs more troops, and that I am worth more as a soldier than a new man would be; I know, too, that the effect of a general re-enlistment upon the rebels will be equal to a victory for us, while it will insure a strong army for the coming campaign." So these men, whom we cannot praise too highly, voluntarily gave three years more of their services to their country. All did not re-enlist. There were many quite as brave and patriotic who could not feel it to be their duty to be longer from their families, but the majority of the young men re-enlisted. Company C bore the palm, furnishing twenty-seven veterans. Company B was next, having twenty-two, then E with eighteen, F with twelve, and little Company D gave eleven. There were not enough from any company to allow any officer to accompany them home, so they were sent home in two squads: one under Sergeant Mader, of Company C, and the other under Sergeant Mason, of Company B. The veterans enjoyed their thirty days' furlough to the fullest extent, lavishing their money with princely hands, and returning promptly to their posts of duty.

Early in March Gen. Dodge extended his command from Athens to Decatur, Alabama, by capturing the latter place early one morning by surprise. The rebel force retreated hastily. This extention of territory required some change in the position of the troops, in consequence of which the 81st Ohio, excepting the three companies at Nance's Mills, were ordered to Lynnville, which place had previously been garrisoned by Col. Bane's brigade. Here again the troops built comfortable quarters in quite neat style, besides preparing a quite formidable stockade.

About the last of January as a couple of wagons were going out from Capt. Overmyer's command at Sam's Mills, for forage, as they were accustomed to do, they were attacked at a brick church on the Shelbyville Pike, about two miles from the mill, by a squad of thirty Confederate cavalry, and as there were but nine men with the wagons, and they totally unprepared for so sudden an attack, they were captured. The rebels burned the two wagons and hurried off with the mules, arms and equipments. Private Mills of Company G was wounded and left. Five men of Company G and three of Company K were captured. As soon as possible Major Evans started in pursuit with a mounted force and very nearly succeeded in overtaking the scoundrels. They paroled their prisoners that night and sent them back, first relieving them of their watches. The rebels knew very well that these paroles were not recognized by us, and the fact that they gave them was but evidence of their great fear for their own safety, which led them to disencumber themselves so readily. The capture of these two wagons, however, seemed to save a larger train of commissary wagons from Pulaski, which the rebels were anxious to get, but which they could not afford to wait for after the noise of this affair.

About the first of April, Captain Gibson, who had for

some time been engaged as superintendent of the mills, in place of Capt. Hill, who had gone North, had the misfortune to become a prisoner of war. He had come to Lynnville on a visit, in company with Major Alman, a citizen, living at Nance's Mills, and as they were returning in the evening, three men suddenly sprang upon them and took them prisoners. They immediately released Major Alman, who went on to the mills and gave the alarm. He had recognized one of the men as the son of a neighbor. Captain Gibson was taken a few miles, relieved of his horse, revolver, watch and three hundred dollars in money. Major Evans started in pursuit and succeeded in recapturing the horse and in establishing the fact that the father of one of the robbers lived in the neighborhood. He was wealthy and was compelled to make good Captain Gibson's loss.

Early in April, the Division commander had telegraphed to Col. Adams to hold his command in readiness to move at a moment's notice, but as no subsequent order was received for a few days, it was thought to be one of the many orders of the kind given for the sake of precaution. The troops were settling down into the belief that they would be consigned for another summer to the easy but inglorious duty of guarding the railroad. But it was not to be so. On the 18th of April, orders came from Division Headquarters for the regiment to move to Pulaski. On the 19th the march was made, a detachment of dismounted cavalry relieving the 81st in the onerous duty of taking care of Lynnville.

But there was little rest at Pulaski. The regiment barely rested there until Col. Adams received orders to take his command to Martin's Plantation, about seven miles distant, for the purpose of putting the fences in repair and guarding the public animals which were to be pastured there. This the boys looked on as a punishment they did not deserve. If guarding railroads was unsuited to their military ardor, what could be expected in the peaceful occupation of a quiet farm, in mending its fences and watching a sickly herd of worn out Government horses and mules! Nevertheless this life had its charms in freedom from military displays, in drill and review, and then the location was pleasant and healthy, and the troops went to work cheerfully to make themselves comfortable. Details were made for guarding the mules that were luxuriating in the rich pasture, and for splitting rails to repair the rickety fences. The latter parties made wonderful progress in the way of felling enormous trees, but did very little toward cutting off the lengths or splitting them into rails. The noise of the falling trees seemed to have charms for them above the pleasures of turning out large numbers of bright new rails.

According to all military precedence, the establishment of this regiment at this place was equivalent to fixing it here for the summer, and accordingly a site was selected with great care for a permanent camping ground, and large details were made to clear it off and put up the tents. The ground was cleared and swept, and the sound of axes and hammers grew clamorous, as, under the hands of the busy workmen the white city was rapidly taking form, when, as if by some stroke of witchery, every hand was dropped, and building up was changed to pulling down. An order had come to move immediately to Pulaski. It was afternoon, but the tents were immediately pulled down and rapidly loaded into wagons, and by four o'clock, on the 26th of April, the regiment, preceded by its excellent drum band which made the woods resonant with "The girl I left behind me," started again toward Pulaski. There was the usual amount of wondering and guessing about what this movement meant, but as all the Government mules and horses were also taken to Pulaski, it was universally conceded that this time there was to be a general movement. After a brisk march, the regiment went into bivouac at Pulaski, and learned that the companies under Major Evans were also ordered in, and that the whole division was under marching orders and would move as soon as the extra baggage could be disposed of. Then ensued a busy time. The accumulated trash of six months' garrison duty was to be cast aside, and the soldiers were to reduce themselves to the lightest marching order. Farewells were to be spoken to those "lights of the camp"—the wives of officers, who, by their presence, had given such a home air to the otherwise forbidding country. Alas! who could tell if this should not be the last farewell?

The day before the departure from Pulaski, the troops were called out to witness the sad sight of the execution of a soldier of the 7th Illinois, who, in 1862, at Corinth had shot his captain. He was tried at the time by Court Martial, and sentenced to death, but the finding and sentence were by some means lost, and the general belief was that they never would be found, but in this the poor man was doomed to disappointment. He was an ill-favored stolid looking man, and seemed to be not at all affected by his impending fate. He marched to the gallows with an air of carelessness and indifference that was positively shocking. A short prayer, a hasty adjustment of the cap and rope—a fall—and all was over.

CHAPTER VIII.

ATLANTA CAMPAIGN—FROM PULASKI TO RESACA.

On the 29th of April, 1864, the troops of the old Second Division of the Sixteenth Army Corps, Army of the Tennessee, again unfurled their banners and marched toward the enemy. Just two years before, they had started from the bloody field of Shiloh, on the then famous campaign against Corinth. It was of a little more than a month's duration, and required a march of not much more than forty miles, including the pursuit to Booneville. What of the coming campaign? Who knows? Will it last a month? It certainly will require more than forty miles of marching, for the nearest enemy in force is two hundred miles away, at Dalton. Ah! it is well, faithful soldier, that you do not know how far you must march—what days of toil and nights of watching await you. And you, fated ones, who are marching to your glorious death on the battle-fields of Georgia, and to your soldier's grave soon to envelop you there, do you ask to know what is in the near future for you? No, no: let the veil, which the beneficent hand of Providence has drawn over the events of the future, rest. You have nobly chosen the soldier's lot; go on, and heroically bear whatsoever burden shall fall to you. If death is yours, you go but earlier to your rest; if life, the gratitude of a whole country will be a perpetual incense, reminding you of the sacrifices you have made.

Gen. Dodge's entire command, known as the Left Wing of the 16th Army Corps, and consisting of the Second Division, commanded by Brig. Gen. Sweeney, and the Fourth Division under command of Brig. Gen. James C. Veatch, moved simultaneously from the various positions in such manner as to concentrate before reaching Chattanooga.

The first day's march was not a difficult one. The ground was a little muddy, but under the inspiriting influence of the splendid drum corps of the regiment, the boys of the 81st tripped gayly through the streets of Pulaski, and out on their unknown journey. Every few miles on the way the drums would beat up, and the scattered and half weary column would at once, as if by magic, spring into order, and taking the cadenced step, would present such a military spectacle as astonished the minds of the rustic and openeyed native beholders. Near night we came to the Elk River, flowing broadly before us, but innocent of ferry or bridge. We had *forded* Bear Creek a year ago, and were not to be discomfited now by this stream. The command "forward!" was given, and the head of the column plunged in, and boldly marched to the opposite shore. The water was about waist deep, and the stream a hundred yards wide. Many never disrobed at all, but most were careful to keep their clothing, as well as their powder, dry. The command bivouacked on the farther shore.

On the next day the march was resumed in the direction of Huntsville, which place we reached on the evening of May 1st. From Huntsville the line of march was along the railroad toward Chattanooga. All along we found deserted camps where the 15th corps had been encamped, which gave us the first intimation that there was to be a grand concentration of troops against the rebel army at Dalton. Early on the morning of the 4th, the Second Division arrived at Larkinsville, Alabama, and there discovered, to the joy of the tired soldiers that cars were in waiting to transport them to Chattanooga. The wagons were all sent over land to Chattanooga under escort of Col. Phillips and his Ninth Illinois mounted infantry.

The embarkation occupied nearly half a day, but shortly after noon the heavy trains got under way. Very soon after leaving Stevenson we began to come in sight of the marching column of the 15th Corps, which, with its long lines of troops and immense wagon train, seemed to stretch from that place almost to Chattanooga. By sunset our trains arrived, and we disembarked and went into bivouac at the base of grand old Lookout Mountain. But notwithstanding the historic associations called up by that eternal monument to the gallantry of our soldiers, there was no time for satisfying curiosity by visiting the interesting place, for early on the 5th the order was again forward, and the troops moved south about nine miles and encamped at Lee & Gordon's Mills, where the first shots in the battle of Chicamauga were fired.

There all day of the 6th was spent in waiting for the 15th corps to get up. The rest was gratefully appreciated by the boys, who spent the day in bathing in the waters of the classic Chicamauga, and in visiting friends in other Ohio regiments in the corps.

On the 7th, McPherson's army moved, taking the road toward Lafayette, but leaving it again and passing that village on the north. The command halted and encamped for the night at Rock Spring, twelve miles from Lee & Gordon's Mills. The next day we reached Snake Creek Gap and moved well down into it that night. So far all was well. We had expected opposition in entering some of these gaps, and had met with none. A couple of rebel scouts had boldly crossed our column on the 8th, between Col. Burke and the front regiment of his brigade, but otherwise we saw not even the signs of where soldiers had been. Gen. Sherman's advance upon the enemy's front at Rocky Face Gap had been so vigorous and demonstrative that Johnston did not suppose it possible that a body of troops could march into Snake Creek Gap.

However, it became known to him about this time that some troops had reached this Gap, and accordingly on the morning of the 9th, as the 16th Corps started toward Resaca with the 9th Illinois mounted infantry in advance, the ball was opened by meeting a rebel force of cavalry which had arrived the previous night to defend the Gap. Col. Phillips with his 9th boldly charged and drove the rebels back, although he received a painful wound in his ankle which sent him north. Infantry skirmishers were sent to the support of the cavalry and the advance was slowly continued, the rebels skirmishing freely as they retired. About three o'clock, as the advance brigade (the 2d) was about one mile and a half from Resaca, a determined fire was opened by the rebels. The brigade was formed in line of battle, and four companies of the 81st Ohio, A, B, C and F, were sent forward as skirmishers. The rest of the Second Division and the Fourth Division were brought up continuing the line to the left. An advance was then made until the skirmish line was within musket shot and in plain view of the rebel fortifications immediately in and about Resaca. Here a halt was called and preparations were made to assault the place. Slowly the hours wore on, but with the exception of occasional bursts of picket firing there was no demonstration made. Private Thomas D. Crossley of Company B, 81st Ohio, was killed about four o'clock by a rebel sharp shooter. He was the first man lost by the regiment in this campaign.

The 15th Corps was close behind the Sixteenth, ready to render support in case it was necessary: the rebel force seemed small—not more than one or two brigades, and yet the order to assault never came. Much censure was expressed concerning Gen. McPherson's course here, and many asked again and again why he did not make the attack when there was such a certainty of success. The following I believe to be the real explanation of his course. In marching out from Snake Creek Gap to Resaca that day, he had crossed a road which leads from Dalton to Rome. It was a good plain road with no obstructions, and as it came from Dalton on the *east* side of those impassable mountains behind which was the remainder of General Sherman's army, it was of course much shorter than one would be from General Sherman to McPherson. Besides, it ran behind General McPherson's position before Resaca, and between him and his safe retreat in Snake Creek Gap. All this of course was known, we presume, in the planning of the campaign, but it was expected that the movement would be a surprise, and it was supposed, too, that Johnston would more tenaciously hold his position at Dalton. His sensitiveness as to the safety of his communications was not then so well known. But just as General McPherson was about to order the assault, he learned that a heavy force of rebels was marching down the Rome road with the intention of cutting him off from Snake Creek Gap, and consequently from the rest of the army. With this knowledge he determined to abandon the attack on Resaca and fall back to the strong defensible position in Snake Creek Gap. Accordingly at dusk the skirmishers were quietly called in, and the whole force, after kindling innumerable sham camp fires, slowly withdrew.

The next morning the 16th Corps was placed in position at the south-west side of the mouth of the Gap, across the Calhoun road. The 15th Corps took position farther to the left, and nearer in the main gap. That night it rained heavily, and just as the heaviest of it was coming down, and when the soldiers had used every artifice to keep dry in order to obtain some sleep, an orderly passed hurriedly through the lines, delivering the hasty and terrible message to company commanders: "Have your command to fall in right away, Johnston with all his force is coming on us!" Ah! "then and there was hurrying to and fro," and waking up of men whose slumbers clung to them as a garment. Despite the dread of meeting "Johnston and all his force," in that plight, it was a very difficult matter to get the soldiers roused and awakened to the use of their faculties. The darkness was opaque and the rain was unremitting, yet one by one the sleepy soldiers were pulled out into line, and at last, when commanders supposed all were ready, the order was given to move. It was laughable next morning to go over the ground occupied by our brigade and see evidences of haste in decamping the night before. Many soldiers had barely awakened in time to go with the troops, and left their guns and accoutrements behind, while others who did not sleep immediately behind their guns were not awakened at all, and only discovered in the morning that their command had gone they knew not where. One or two officers had the misfortune to forget their swords and field glasses. Every article of soldier's use, nearly, was found next morning among the abandoned articles. One company of the 81st Ohio was left on picket duty on the line which the brigade left, and they found themselves well supported in the morning by the unfortunate men of the command who had lost portions of their property. The brigade had only moved back a mile, into the mouth of the Gap, where, with the rest of the Corps and in conjunction with the 15th Corps, an extensive line of earthworks was commenced.

CHAPTER IX.

ATLANTA CAMPAIGN—FROM SNAKE CREEK GAP TO LAY'S FERRY.

All day of the 11th of May, spades and picks were busy in the construction of this, the first ditch of the campaign. All day the troops confidently and patiently awaited the approach of Johnston and all his force, but in vain. The army had not yet learned the caution of that General, or they would not have been troubled about his coming. Instead of Johnston, the troops soon had the pleasure of seeing the advance of the Army of the Cumberland coming through the Gap. Leaving Schofield to hold Johnston at Rocky Face, Sherman was massing to defeat him at Resaca. All day of the 12th the long lines of the 20th and 14th Corps came through and beyond our lines and encamped in the broad fields before us. Gen. Sherman and Gen. Thomas also came upon the scene, and it was evident that something important was to be done.

By night of the 12th, there was massed in the low ground at the mouth of Snake Creek Gap, such a force as few had seen so near together before during the war. Their camp fires that chilly night, formed a scene of indescribable beauty and grandeur which was not untouched by a tinge of melancholy interest as one looked upon it and knew that a great battle would be fought next day, and that many now cheerful and happy beside these fires, would to-morrow night be all cold and lifeless on the battle-field!

Early on the morning of the 13th, every thing was astir. Cavalry flocked to the front and heavy masses of infantry moved after, and the artillery jostled on to its day's work of death. Soon the left of the army became engaged near

Resaca. As the day wore on, the battle rolled from our left toward the right, but did not reach the extreme right where the 16th Corps was posted, except the brigade commanded by Col. Sprague. The brigade to which the 81st Ohio belonged moved slowly nearly all day, going into line of battle several times, and finally bivouacking within one mile of Resaca at night, without having engaged in the fight. Almost all day the battle had raged with varying severity on our left, including the 15th Corps which lay almost immediately on the left of the 16th. At nightfall we could plainly see the railroad south of Resaca, where train after train was seen going out, evidently carrying away wounded and stores, preparatory to an evacuation.

The next day, 14th, was the final day of the battle of Resaca, but as the 81st had another duty to perform, away from the main battle-field, my pen will follow its movements. Early on the morning of the 14th, Gen. Sweeney's Division of Gen. Dodge's command was ordered to Lay's Ferry, where Snake Creek empties into the Oostenaula river. This is some six miles from Resaca, and five from Calhoun—a town some four miles south of Resaca, on the railroad to Atlanta. It was determined by General Sherman to lay a pontoon bridge over the Oostenaula at this point, in order that a force could be hurled against Johnston's flank and rear, in case he should determine to retreat. The important duty of laying this pontoon in the face of the enemy was assigned to Gen. Sweeney's Division. While the 3d brigade was instructed to make demonstrations at Calhoun Ferry, between Resaca and Lay's Ferry, the other two brigades proceeded to the latter place.

The Oostenaula is a deep, narrow, rapid stream, running at this ferry through banks not more than twenty feet high. On each side the land rises, at a distance of about three hundred yards, thirty feet more, and then runs back a level plain for a long distance. On the rebel side of the river the road was bordered on the lower side by a dense forest; on the upper side by an open field. On the Union side the road to the ferry ran for the last mile through open fields. A hundred yards below the ferry and opposite the forest spoken of was the mouth of Snake Creek, a stream twenty feet wide and two or three feet deep, with precipitous banks. To move down the road to the ferry through those open fields in the face of the enemy would be almost impossible, as the crossing was defended by Jackson's rebel brigade of cavalry, with entrenchments, and aided by a battery of artillery under cover. It was determined to make the crossing at the mouth of Snake Creek, where the deep forest and the line of trees along its bank afforded a slight screen to hide our movements. In the mean time, however, very vigorous efforts were apparently made to force a way to the river along the road, in order to attract the enemy's attention from our real movements. A line of skirmishers, consisting of the 66th Illinois was pushed clear to the river, and Welker's Battery was stationed in an open field without cover of any sort to play against the rebel battery. The pontoon trains were then unloaded at the cross roads, a mile from the ferry, but the nearest they could be brought without being seen by the rebels. The pontoon boats, which consisted of wooden frames, very light but firm, and covered with strong white canvas, were unloaded and put in order. Their appearance as defensive vessels of war was any thing but satisfactory to the soldiers who anticipated a chance of being detailed to cross the river in them. The boys called them "canvas ironclads," "muslin ships," and other names not indicative of implicit trust in their defensive qualities. The 7th Iowa regiment was detailed to perform the laborious task of carrying these boats to the river, or as near it as practicable. The 81st Ohio and 12th Illinois accompanied as a support. About twenty men were assigned to each boat. Bearing the boats aloft on their shoulders and walking as near the shelter of the trees along the banks of Snake Creek as they could, the procession started.

Meantime it had been discovered that the rebel skirmish line extended down the bank of the river below the mouth of Snake Creek where we intended to cross, and that it would be impossible to carry the boats all the way to the river. It was then determined to carry them as far down Snake Creek as possible, and then under cover of the bank of that stream launch the boats in it, man them, row down to the mouth and boldly strike across the Oostenaula, and drive the rebels from the opposite shore. Then, when the main force at the ferry had been thus flanked and driven away, the boats could be towed up to the ferry and the bridge made at the desired place. But here a difficulty presented itself; Snake Creek was not deep enough to float the boats until within a hundred yards of its mouth, and there the rebel sharpshooters had full control—the artillery and weak line of skirmishers being unavailing to drive them off. It was determined to send the 81st Ohio and 12th Illinois down to the bank to reinforce the skirmishers, and under cover of a vigorous musketry fire from these two regiments, the boats were to be rapidly launched. As the rebels saw these regiments approaching, they redoubled their fire, and as there was a wide open field to cross before reaching the river bank, the troops were ordered forward double-quick. Catching the inspiration of a charge, as the soldiers quickened their pace they raised their voices, and with a yell that would have done credit to a whole tribe of Camanches, the 81st Ohio and 12th Illinois rushed across the field and dropped behind the fence and bushes on the bank of the river; and such a firing as then ensued! The rebels, with a strong skirmish line, were just across the narrow river behind the trees, while we, with a skirmish line and a line of battle, let loose volley after volley at them. The fire was warmly returned and their spiteful balls struck thickly among the rails and on the ground, while here and there some poor fellow was wounded or killed. While this close and deafening firing was in progress, the rebels were so much occupied by it that our boats were safely launched. Still the rebels were not to be scared away, and there was nothing left but the last dangerous resort of boldly pushing a force across and storming the bank.

Who should cross first? There were not wanting brave men who would willingly volunteer for such a duty, but volunteers were not called for. Upon whom was this lot of danger, and possibly of honor to fall? It was the original plan, I believe, to send across the 66th Illinois and support them with other troops, but as they had already been heavily engaged in skirmishing, and had spent much of their ammunition, the order had to be changed. One company of the 66th, however, which had been in reserve, and two companies of the 81st Ohio, B and C, were ordered to embark in the "muslin ships" which had already been launched in Snake Creek. These companies had to be divided in embarking, as the boats would hold but eighteen or twenty men each. These three companies being safely embarked and the rebels making but little disturbance, it was determined to fill the remaining boats and let them follow closely to assist in case of need. But chance at last decided who should cross first, for the boats had become somewhat mixed up in the embarking, and when all was ready, Lieut. Colonel Adams, to whom had been entrusted the delicate duty of superintending the first crossing of troops, directed the first three boats to move down the stream and cross. The order in which they lay when the order was given, gave the advance to Lieut. Geo. W. Dixon, with a platoon of Co. B, 81st Ohio; next was Capt. Hays, with a platoon of Co. I. 66th Illinois, and third, Capt. W. H. Chamberlin, with a platoon of Co. C, 81st Ohio. The command of these three boats and of the skirmishers when they should land, was given to the latter officer. All was at last ready; the detailed instructions to each platoon were given. Before those brave men loomed a dark deep forest which might prove to them a magazine of death! At its edge flowed the angry, rapid Oostenaula, perhaps soon to be crimsoned by their life-blood. Yet from this possible fate not a man shrank, though many a heart stood still a moment, and many a thought of home and dear ones came up as for a last retrospect.

The order was given for the three boats to proceed. Silently the oarsmen from the Pioneer Corps of the Army of the Cumberland, who had taken thus the advance of that army across the Tennessee at Caperton Ferry, and who rowed Sherman across to assist in the battle of Chattanooga, but who had never yet made a crossing in the immediate face of the enemy, dipped their long oars into the muddy waters of Snake Creek and moved the boats toward the river. Not a word is spoken, except a few hurried injunctions from the leading oarsmen to the others to keep time and pull together. As still as death, the white boats, with their living cargoes of blue move on down Snake Creek. They have nearly reached the river when a startling voice from the rear cries out—"halt!" The hindmost two of the boats hear the order and stop, but the foremost does not, and is already out in the river, where to stop or attempt to turn back would be certain death; while to go forward, alone, would be simply to go deliberately as prisoners. Shall the gallant little crew be abandoned to its fate? There is no way to get it back, and it cannot go on in safety. What shall be done? Col. Adams quickly decided to order forward the other two boats. Obeying the order without questioning why, they sped forward into the river. The first boat was now nearly across, the second had reached the middle of the stream, but the third, on entering the river had struck on a snag! At this juncture the rebels appeared to have first discovered the movement, and plash! plash! into the water came the balls around the third boat! Happily it was easily got adrift, and bending to their oars right gallantly, those sturdy oarsmen sped the little boat like a dart through that gauntlet of Death! Almost simultaneously with the first three boats came the fourth and fifth, bringing the remainder of Companies B and C, 81st Ohio, under Lieutenants Miller and Irion. It was the work of but a moment to deploy those willing soldiers along the bank, and then with a bound and a yell and a volley, to spring up the bank and scatter the astonished rebels like sheep. In almost as brief a space of time as it takes to write it, the gallant little band had captured almost as large a body of prisoners, including one captain and two lieutenants. The main rebel force on the left at the ferry, finding themselves outflanked by an unknown number of Yankees—for they could see nothing of our operations, and could only judge by the yelling, which was participated in by the rest of the Division—took to flight for safety. Some of the fleeter footed of our skirmishers were in time to overtake some of them and take them prisoners. Three men of Company C, 81st Ohio, John M. Henness, Samuel T. Wiley, and James E. J. Dill, took eleven rebels prisoners in one squad, including one captain and two lieutenants. By this time the boats had been busy in bringing over re-enforcements, consisting of Companies A, E, F, and H, 81st Ohio, two companies of the 66th Illinois, and one from the 12th Illinois—all under command of Captain

W. H. Hill, 81st Ohio, and the little band that had first landed felt no further apprehensions for their safety. Several times the rebels gathered their forces, and attempted to make a charge, but our boys bravely met them with a volley and a cheer, and drove them back. The peril of the crossing being passed and complete success crowning the movement so far, it was with a feeling of bitter disappointment that the troops received the order about sunset to withdraw, and re-cross the river. Soon after sunset the troops were all safely across the river, and so demoralized and frightened were the enemy that they did not discover our withdrawal in time to fire a shot at us. Thus ended the first passage of the Oostenaula by Sherman's army.

It will afford but little consolation to the brave men who participated in it, or to the friends of those whose blood dyed that river, to know that a delay of one minute in starting the first boat would have been sufficient to have prevented the crossing of any of them. Gen. McPherson had received information that a large rebel force was crossing at Calhoun ferry between us and the main army, for the evident purpose of cutting off Gen. Sweeney's Division. He immediately dispatched a courier to Gen. Sweeney, telling him to delay the crossing until the truth or falsity of the rumor could be ascertained. This courier arrived and the order to cross was countermanded just too late to be heard by the first boat, as above stated, and then the remaining boats crossed merely to save the crew of that one. The rumor about the enemy crossing proved false, but it was not ascertained in time to lay the pontoons that night, and hence the troops were withdrawn.

The crossing was not effected without loss. In the fourth boat that crossed, Sergeant Crothers and Private John M. Wiley, 81st Ohio, and one of the oarsmen, were instantly killed. Sergeant Baird, 81st Ohio, had captured three rebels, and was just marching them off, when a rebel officer appeared and threatened to shoot them if they did not seize their guns and fire on Baird; they obeyed and shot him, severely wounding him about the head and leaving him for dead. A number of others were wounded, and one, Private David Y. Lyttle, was captured, having, in his eagerness to capture prisoners, ventured too far forward.

During this day and night, while these operations were in progress, on the extreme right, the main part of Sherman's army was engaged heavily at and around Resaca. Far into the night, the sullen boom of the cannon and the rattle of musketry told of the fierce conflict in progress there. Saturday morning brought the news of the evacuation of Resaca, and the retreat of Johnston's whole army southward. Oh! then for the pontoon bridge which *might* have been laid at Lay's Ferry the previous day. Such a staggering blow as could be directed against the retreating enemy from this road! But as the bridge was not already there, the next best thing was to put it there as quickly as possible, and General Sweeney's command again undertook it. This time the rebels seemed less determined, and a strong demonstration being made against them they fled from the river bank and allowed the peaceable laying of the bridge at Lay's Ferry, just where it was wanted. As soon as it was in a condition to bear footmen, the infantry of the first brigade crossed and took position along the river bank on the right. The second followed and formed on the left of the road along the bank. For some reason, the forwarding of more troops seemed delayed, as was the preparation of the bridge. No artillery crossed on that day, and no advance by the infantry was made. A skirmish line was thrown forward, which soon discovered a rebel force in position. In fact we could see their skirmishers in the farther edge of the field. In the evening, as soon as our skirmishers made a slight advance, the

rebels essayed a charge, and did emerge from the woods
in good line with guns at a right shoulder shift. On they
came with nothing apparently to oppose them but the
thin line of skirmishers, for they could not see the troops
of the first brigade which had been thrown forward behind
a slight elevation on the right of the road. Suddenly
their easy progress was arrested by our remorseless shell
thrown from Welker's battery with unerring certainty,
from the other side of the river, and bursting with terrible
effect plump among them. Almost at the same time a
blinding volley from our infantry, behind the elevation,
came into their faces. Their line halted in sheer consternation—then wavered—rallied and fired a weak volley—
wavered again, and then melted away, leaving traces of
its position in the blood of the wounded and the bodies of
the slain. So plainly in sight of the second brigade was
this little battle, that although out of ordinary range, the
boys could not resist having a " pop" at them. The rebel
lines were near enough for some of their balls to reach us.
One man of the 66th Illinois was killed here, and Color-
Sergeant, John A. Wilson, 81st Ohio, received a painful
wound while defiantly waving his flag at the enemy.

CHAPTER X.

ATLANTA CAMPAIGN—FROM LAY'S FERRY TO BIG SHANTY.

That night the Second Division lay at the Ferry, and after night threw up defensive works—a precaution which proved entirely unnecessary. The next day the remaining portion of the corps was ordered up, and the bridge being completed, the artillery was crossed over, and at 10 o'clock General Sweeney's Division again started forward. At the distance of a mile or two we came upon a strong defensive position of the rebels which was abandoned, showing that retreat was in progress. About one o'clock, our skirmishers became engaged with the rebels, and it was soon ascertained that Cleburne's and Walker's divisions of the rebel army were posted there to protect a wagon train which was passing along a road beyond one known as the Rome road. General Dodge arrived about this time and gave personal attention to the disposition of the troops. Without knowing anything definitely of the enemy's strength or position save what was gathered from the fact that his skirmish line was very long, it was impossible to make a close formation with a single Division. The 4th Division had not yet come up. General Dodge placed the first brigade on the left of the road, facing eastwardly. Then with an interval between, the third brigade was placed on the right of the first, facing to the north-east, while still farther to the right and facing north, was the second brigade. Our long line of skirmishers was continually engaged, especially on the right. General McPherson himself rode along the lines, and as the rebel troops were too strong for this one Division, and as the remainder of the 16th Corps, followed by the 15th Corps, were coming up, as rapidly as possible, he ordered that the enemy should not be pressed. Two hours of skirmishing ensued, when our boys on the right of the line, becoming impatient, and being under command of the restless Captain George A. Taylor, 66th Illinois, advanced slightly, and drove the rebel skirmishers from their position, beyond the Rome road. Captain Taylor, on reaching this road, and seeing a party of rebels fleeing down it, took a few men with him and started in pursuit. Reckless of life, he followed, until suddenly a volley from a party in ambush burst upon him, and he fell, dead—shot through the brain. The death of Captain Taylor had such a disheartening effect on his men that they began to yield, gradually, the ground they had gained. Almost the entire regiment of sharpshooters, (66th Illinois) was deployed as skirmishers, and three companies of the 81st Ohio, under Captain Hill, were sent out to support them. Holding the rebels with this long line, and waiting for the 4th Division to come up, the time was passing, while but little progress was made. Perceiving that we did not attack, and perhaps thinking we were weak, the enemy began to press our lines. Stronger and stronger became the firing on the right, until it was evident that their attack would be at that place.

Colonel Burke, our brigade commander, went forward to learn as well as possible the nature of the ground and the position of the enemy. It was almost all a dense forest filled thickly with a dense undergrowth of pine, and it was impossible to ascertain anything except by hearing. Both General McPherson and General Dodge now appeared at the right and the former directed that the right should be refused a little. Although the enemy was hidden from view, and the balls were thickly striking among the trees, General Dodge rode forward to the advanced line and gave directions in person as to its position. The attack was coming directly on the right flank of the second brigade, and its regiments were disposed thus: the 66th Illinois was scattered along a mile of skirmish line. The 81st Ohio was divided into three battalions, each separated some distance from the others. The 12th Illinois on the left of the 81st was almost intact—one or two companies perhaps on the skirmish line. To meet the exigency of a charge on the flank, the battalion of the 81st Ohio, under Major Evans, was ordered to change front so as to face to the east toward the Rome road. Hardly was this accomplished until the rebels, pressing in the skirmishers, began the attack on the two right battalions of the 81st Ohio, under Lieutenant-Colonel Adams and Captain Hill. The latter being on the extreme right was soon enveloped by the enemy, and compelled to fall back and join Colonel Adams' battalion. The 12th Illinois was now hurried forward and to the right, to fill the gap between Major Evans' battalion and the others of the 81st Ohio. About this time, Major Evans, who had been ordered to hold that valley until further orders, perceived a line of rebels bearing down upon him. Relying on the tried gallantry of his command, without stopping to think how many were in his front, he ordered a charge. With a resounding cheer the men rose, and, as one man, moved resistlessly forward over logs and through thick pine brush, stopping for no obstacles. Volley after volley they sent, too, rattling through the trees among the rebel ranks, as the line kept advancing. By this time, too, the 12th on the right came up, and it, with the remaining battalions of the 81st, still farther on the right, sent so many balls through those almost impenetrable woods, and raised such unearthly shouts, that the rebel hearts failed, and they ignobly fled. The brigade carried the pursuit some distance, so far, indeed, that a part of Major Evans' battalion found an enemy immediately on its left flank, and quickly changing front, and having advantage of position, drove them from the field.

In the mean time, the third brigade was menaced. One of its batteries being in a somewhat advanced position, was coveted by some sharp-shooters who attempted to capture it. A vigorous shelling was given also to that part of the line, some of the shells bursting far in our rear, and raising an incipient panic among some casual teams, ambulances and caissons passing along the road, but no serious attack was made except on the second brigade.

As it was now late, and the 4th Division had come up, it was determined to withdraw the Second Division and relieve it with the fourth. The withdrawal was done easily, as from subsequent events we may infer that the enemy was quite anxious to give us no trouble as long as we did not molest him. In fact the attack was only made to cover a hasty movement in retreat of their wagon trains, and there was no disposition to take the offensive. They were perfectly satisfied to be let alone, as they were, from nearly sunset. This may account for their feeble defense, and the consequent small loss inflicted on our troops, which did not exceed seventy-five.

Colonel P. E. Burke, of the 66th Illinois, was here wounded, and, in consequence, soon after lost his life. He was in the front from the beginning. Early in the engagement a ball struck his left leg below the knee and shattered the bone. He rode up to Lieutenant-Colonel Adams, and quietly remarking that he was wounded, turned over the command of the brigade to that officer, and rode away. His leg was amputated and he was started north to recover, but gangrene supervening, his death ensued before he could leave Georgia.

During the short time that he had commanded the brigade he had endeared himself to his entire command by his gentlemanly courtesy and uniform kindness. By his gallant bearing in the field, every soldier was constrained to repose the fullest confidence in his bravery, and his death was deeply and sincerely lamented by his command. Lieutenant-Colonel Adams succeeded to the command of the brigade, and Major Evans had command of the 81st Ohio.

This engagement, fought on the 16th of May, 1864, was known as the battle of Rome Cross Roads.

The next three days witnessed the grand beginning of the great race southward of the two armies. I say the beginning, for although Sherman halted purposely at Kingston, to replenish his stock of supplies, he did not again come in determined contact with the enemy until he found him at Dallas. Late on the evening of the 17th of May, the 16th Corps started forward in the direction of the enemy, southward. The whole army, indeed, was also in motion. By various roads the interminable lines of blue, dotted with the almost numberless white-covered army wagons, were moving almost without cessation night and day toward an enemy. Before noon of the 19th, the advance of General Sherman's army entered Kingston, driving out the rebel rear-guard. On the 18th, eleven engines and trains, under Confederate control, lay there, and late in the evening moved south with the army. Before daylight of the 20th, a Yankee engineer sounded the whistle that heralded the approach of the first engine under Federal direction. As the roar of the whistle re-echoed through those mountains, it received a gladsome welcome in the answering shouts of the thousands of troops who literally swarmed all over the ground. The boys often facetiously remarked, in view of the close following up of the rebels by our railroad trains, that General Johnston traveled on a train just in advance of General Sherman, and that the former kept his train flagged to keep Sherman from running into him! Through the entreaties of Governor Brown, who was anxious to save the property of the State, the Confederates did very little damage to the road, as they retreated, and General Sherman could thus keep his trains up with his army.

The 81st Ohio had three good days of rest on a green grassy hill-side, at Kingston, while a portion of the army advanced a few miles and skirmished with the enemy. During these three days, General Sherman's untiring energy, infused into his subordinates, had brought forward twenty days' supplies for the entire army, and he was ready again to assume the defensive.

While we were lying at Kingston, Colonel Mersey, 9th Illinois, returned, and, by virtue of seniority, took command of the brigade—Colonel Adams returning to the command of the 81st Ohio.

The enemy had halted at the Etowah river, and, on the 19th, Gen. Johnston had issued a battle order to his troops, announcing that he would now turn and lead them against the foe, and exhorting them to acquit themselves valiantly. Prisoners afterward taken said that the order was scarcely read to some of the regiments until the inevitable order to fall back came, and the enemy crossed the river. Here, then, was not only the river in their front, but the Allatoona Pass was in their possession—an admirable defensive position. To dislodge them, General Sherman again determined on a flank movement, and again he ordered McPherson to the right, to lead the flanking force. This time it fell to the lot of the 81st Ohio to form a part of the rear of the column, on the starting out. They were to follow after the wagon trains. Never, perhaps, did they have so unpleasant a verification of the adage that "large bodies move slowly," as on the present occasion. Early in the morning of the 23d, orders were given to be ready to march at a moment's notice, but the morning wore away and left the troops lying as the sunrise had found them.

At noon the glad sound of "fall in" was heard, for every soldier dreaded the prospect of a night march, which was sure to come if they did not start soon. Still the great parks of wagons were slowly winding out into the roads, and the troops had to halt very soon after starting. It seemed as if the last wagon would never come. Sadly enough the troops saw the sun declining, and knew they were doomed to a night march—a thing more perplexing and troublesome than almost anything else a soldier had to undergo. It was actually sunset when the last of the troops left Kingston, and a night march, of course, followed. Tired with the whole day's tedious waiting, and then, to follow a long wagon train, after night, was the acme of a soldier's misery. There is nothing more trying to the patience than marching after a wagon train. Moving forward ten feet, perhaps, there is an unexplained halt of two minutes, then another forward, double-quick, for a hundred yards, then a halt of half an hour, and so on, with variations as to time and distance, until the most patient heartily wishes there was no such thing as a mule, or a wheel, connected with the army. Plunging into gutters, tumbling over stumps and stones, running eyes plump against the muzzle of the gun of a careless file-leader, getting notice to halt only by blundering against the man in advance, and being in turn blundered against by the man behind; covered, enveloped, penetrated, body and clothes, with the dirty, gray mist of dust, two inches deep on the ground, is it any wonder that the soldiers dreaded a night march? But this was the lot of the 81st Ohio that night. At midnight they got into camp, and soon forgot all their discomforts in sleep, such as only the soldier can appreciate.

On the 24th, McPherson's command encamped at Van Wert, a little village some twenty miles south-west of Kingston, and apparently far removed from all military operations. From Van Wert the line of march was changed toward Dallas, which place was entered, after slight skirmishing, simultaneously by McPherson's force and by General Jeff. C. Davis' division of the 14th Corps. That night, as some of the troops were going into bivouac, they were fired into, and the next morning it was a matter of some surprise to many to find that the rebel army was lying close in our front, and that a great battle might be fought that day. But either the rebels were themselves too weak, or were unadvised of our lengthened line, and they did not press their advantage. Accordingly the 27th was occupied in stretching out our troops in the most defensible positions, and, at the same time, pressing the enemy as much as possible. The 81st Ohio was called out to form a part of the skirmish line, but, in the course of the movement, it was crowded out, and remained in reserve. The day's work was one of the most severe and extended skirmishes we had then known. At night our troops had gained some good positions, and fortifications were hastily thrown up. The 15th Corps was on the right of the 14th, and formed the extreme right of the army. On the left of the 16th was Davis' division of the 14th Corps; then a gap, and then the Army of the Cumberland and of the Ohio.

All day of the 28th there was heavy skirmishing. The rattling musketry, and occasional hoarse notes of the artillery, betokened enough of battle to keep a slow procession of ambulances passing between the front and the hospitals to convey the wounded. Toward evening an unusual activity appeared among the rebels in front of General Logan's right. A storm was coming, where should it break? The attempt to turn Logan's flank was only a ruse. Minor attacks were made all along the line of the 15th Corps, but the main effort was to be made against General Dodge's command. Bates' Division of Hardee's Corps was hurled against Sweeney's Division, which, at that time, presented a front of two regiments and one portion of a battery. The immortal 2d Iowa, and the younger, but not less gallant, 66th Indiana, with two sections of Captain Welker's Battery, (H, 1st Missouri Light Artillery,) met the shock of the charge. Fierce and hot was the contest--brave men were pitted against brave--but it was impossible to advance before the withering fire of that gallant line of Colonel Rice's brigade. In half an hour from the time the first volley was fired, the shout of victory rang on the evening air, and was taken up by regiment after regiment, until the woods was vocal with rejoicings. So determined were the rebels in the assaulting columns, that several actually forced themselves over our works, where they were at once captured. The Kentucky troops formed a part of the assaulting column. The loss of the 66th Illinois and the 2d Iowa was very slight, but sixty-three dead rebels were counted in our front the next day.

On the morning of the 29th, Colonel Mersey's brigade relieved Colonel Rice's, and the 81st Ohio had a taste of what it was to man those works. Company B was sent out on the skirmish line, and private James Anderson, of Company D, being desirous to have an adventure, volunteered to go also. He was permitted to go, but in an hour his dead body was borne back. All day the heavy skirmishing was kept up. The lines were so close that the troops behind the works were compelled to keep down, or have a rebel bullet in unpleasant proximity to their ears. Indeed the balls went as far back as the headquarters of Generals Dodge and Sweeney.

It appears that General McPherson had marched too rapidly, and had got too far to the right, in taking this position at Dallas, and it was necessary to draw him farther to the left, so as to join more closely to the rest of the army. Orders had been issued on the 28th of May for him to withdraw a few miles toward his left, but this attack by the enemy caused the order to be countermanded. It was again issued on the 29th. All the teams had moved during the afternoon and evening, (except advance wagons) and, at dark, the reserve artillery began moving. After it the artillery and infantry from the extreme right were to silently move off, continuing the movement toward the left, only leaving the skirmish line on duty, which was to follow at day-light.

The movement was in progress. The loud rattle of the rtillery certainly could be heard in the rebel camps on that clear still night. At about eleven o'clock at night, when some of us were listening to the dull booming of Hooker's cannon, away to the left, the bright flash of a musket to the right, and in front of our line, told of approaching danger. Almost instantly the whole picket line, in front of Mersey's brigade, was ablaze and retiring. The sound of their guns awakened the men who were sleeping in the trenches. Scarcely had the retiring pickets reached the works until every man in the long sinuous line, which a moment before seemed wrapped in slumber, was up to his place. "What is it?" was hurriedly asked, as the pickets clambered over the works. "The enemy— a charge!" was the whispered reply, and in an instant the 81st Ohio and the 12th Illinois poured a volley of death into the advancing column. An irregular line of flashes among the trees, and a legion of mad bullets whizzing over our heads, was the reply. A section of Welker's battery, on the left of the 81st Ohio, now lit up the whole scene with its vivid breath of flame, while its reports shook the earth. It was such a scene as few of us will ever see again. The firing of the infantry became constant, but irregular, after the first volley, while to its timid and sinuous line of light was added, every moment, the glare of one or more of Welker's guns, which seemed to be discharging their death missiles without cessation. That grand old forest at the romantic hour of midnight, never before resounded to such unearthly din. The sulphurous smoke from the guns seemed to hang about the earth, so that the darkness was changed to gray, in which the dark figures of the men became visible—a sort of demon-looking set, engaged in a ghastly play with death! There was too much of death in it to be long continued by the rebels, and they fell back—exactly when, we could not tell, for once started, some of the boys could not be induced to cease firing. However, there was a silence at last, but of brief duration, for on our right was a clash and clatter heard, where the rebels assayed to break the lines of the 15th Corps. Maddened, as it were, they again burst upon Mersey's line, to be again driven back. Again, and again, at different points, they made efforts, until by three A. M., there had been seven distinct assaults upon our lines.

The loss was mostly on the part of the enemy, they having all the disadvantage of making the attack at a time when it was impossible to see their object, or to keep their troops in order. The testimony of a rebel prisoner, captured a day or two afterward, was, that Bates' Division was cut to pieces in that attack, which, he said, was made by a misunderstanding of orders.

During the course of the first firing, some of the more excitable men managed to lose in part, and shoot away in part, their ammunition, until, in five or ten minutes, their cartridge-boxes were exhausted, and they began to call lustily for ammunition. Unfortunately, in consequence of the movement which was in progress, almost all the ammunition wagons were gone, and quite all were gone from the front line. In this emergency red tape was cut effectually. Failing to find the proper ordnance officer, in the melee, which would have been almost impossible, General Dodge hailed the first wagons he saw containing ordnance, only satisfying himself that they contained the proper caliber, and, although they belonged to another Corps, he ordered them unloaded at once. Seizing a box of canister himself, and placing it before him on his horse, the General started to the front, and in this useful style presented himself to the astonished gunners of Welker's battery. By the efforts of staff officers, a full supply of ammunition was soon, almost miraculously at hand, and all apprehensions on this score were set at rest.

From three o'clock we had undisturbed rest, and some time before noon of the 30th, the 81st and 12th were relieved, and allowed to enjoy a slight respite at a point in the safe distance. So, sleeping and resting, the remainder of the 30th was spent, while the proposed movement was held in abeyance, and the rebels were non-plussed by our unbroken front. Their attack on the night of the 29th had evidently been made with a view to pierce our lines while we were moving, and, taking advantage of the confusion which they supposed would follow, they hoped to do us much mischief. The only fault was, that their attack was made too soon. An hour or two later, we might have been in motion, and the result might have been quite different. As it was, General McPherson found it no easy matter to let go his hold on the rebel tiger which he had so easily caught. Still he was patient. All day of the 30th his lines doggedly held their ground.

The 31st of May was a repetition of the 30th, except that little demonstrations were made, here and there, against the enemy, for effect. One of these occurred in General Sweeney's Division. That officer was ordered by General Dodge to make a reconnoisance in his front, to ascertain if the enemy was still in force there; but he was in no wise to make an assault, as he would be unsupported by either the forces on his right or left. But, being, perhaps, ambitious to do something brilliant, General Sweeney ordered Col-

9

onel Mersey to take his Brigade and make an assault on the enemy's works. The order was obeyed, and partly carried out, when General Dodge arrived on the field and ordered the Brigade withdrawn. The 66th Illinois, in this movement, formed the skirmish line, and lost a number in killed and wounded. By good luck, the 81st Ohio met with no loss, although it crossed the works in line of battle. Even if the assault had been made, and had been successful, there was not the least good that could have accrued from it, for of what avail would it have been to break a few hundred yards of a line, miles in length, by a little detached force, acting without the co-operation, or even the knowledge, of the rest of the army. It would have been but an empty honor at the best.

That night the regiment, with the rest of the Brigade, received marching orders soon after dark, and moved, about ten o'clock, toward the left. It was nearly daylight when the wearied troops arrived at their destination, and found that the Brigade was to relieve a portion of General Davis' Division, which had already vacated the works and moved farther to the left, to join the rest of the Corps. The 12th Illinois was sent out to the picket line, said to be a mile distant, while the 81st Ohio, and the 66th Illinois were thinly scattered along a long line of earthworks. It was no permanent occupation, but was only done to make a show of front, while the rest of McPherson's command was moved farther to the left. Foiled in all his previous attempts at withdrawal, he attempted it again on the night of the 31st of May, and, by good fortune, succeeded in making the movement, unmolested, during the night. It was nearly noon before the rebels discovered the movement, and entered the town of Dallas, which had been in rear of our lines. At this time, Colonel Mersey's Brigade, stretched out thus in single file, was the extreme right of our army—the rest having moved to the new position assigned, some two or three miles from that recently occupied. With no cavalry to watch his flank and rear, Colonel Mersey quietly awaited orders for his own withdrawal, while, without his knowledge, the rebel cavalry were advancing through Dallas, and down in his rear. At the same time, the enemy's infantry could be seen, feeling its way toward his flank, and pressing on toward his front. The first intimation he had of the presence of the enemy in his rear, was given in the report of carbines at a very short distance. Sending out an additional short line of skirmishers on the right flank, which soon became warmly engaged with the enemy's skirmishers, Colonel Mersey bent back his right, until what remained of the 66th Illinois, and 81st Ohio formed a line of battle, facing toward nearly all the points of the compass. The Colonel knew now that he was entirely isolated from the army, and that he was almost entirely surrounded, but he determined to stay there and fight it out, until he should receive orders to withdraw, or be defeated and captured. At last, when his little handful of men seemed just on the point of being transformed into a mouthful for the delectation of the Confederate maw, the order to withdraw came, and marching the 12th Illinois as skirmishers on his (now) right, he dextrously withdrew his little command without loss, and received the congratulations of his superior officers.

Before nightfall, the entire command of General McPherson had built substantial earthworks, and rested from their labors, out of hearing of the incessant sound of the skirmisher's gun. The next day or two was spent in strengthening our works, and in rest. The enemy seemed nonplussed. We could see evident signs of a hurried movement toward their right. This movement of General McPherson's army betokened some danger in that direction

General Sherman had, by moving to this position at Dallas, already drawn most of the enemy away from the railroad and the strong position at Allatoona. It only remained for him to quietly march his army back to that point, and possess it. This was the next movement. On the 5th and 6th of June, the march to Acworth on the railroad, several miles south of Allatoona, was made. Here, the main portion of the army had another rest of several days, during which McPherson's command was reinforced by the arrival of the 17th Corps. While a show of attack was kept up, Sherman rested his army, and rebuilding the railroad bridge over the Etowah River, soon had the "cracker line," as the soldiers familiarly called it, re-established. Clothing and abundant supplies were issued, and on the 10th of June the Army of the Tennessee moved down the railroad as far as Big Shanty.

Here we came in sight of the inevitable enemy again, intrenched, in front of Kennesaw Mountain. From the 10th till the 15th of June, the 81st did nothing but lie in bivouac. The Army of the Tennessee was engaged in this time in slowly forming its line closer and closer upon the enemy's works. It now formed the extreme left of the whole army. The wet weather made approaches difficult, but on the 15th the lines were advanced about two miles south of Big Shanty, and the rebel works, built about a mile in front of Kennesaw Mountain, were close in the Union front. During this approach, and after its completion, there was a repetition of the same endless skirmish firing, which had been the rule at Dallas, varied, occasionally, by a heavy cannonade, and, now and then, a short, sharp contest, where volleys of musketry told of a little charge.

CHAPTER XI.

ATLANTA CAMPAIGN—FROM BIG SHANTY TO KENNESAW MOUNTAIN.

Kennesaw Mountain, though a detached, abrupt elevation, of not more than a half mile in length, and apparently indefensible, proved to be one of the most formidable natural barriers we had to contend with. It was sufficiently near to Lost Mountain to make it possible, with the large army the rebels had, to continue the line across the low country between, and thus take advantage of both elevations. While Kennesaw formed the rebel right, Lost Mountain formed the left. The chief advantage gained by the possession of Kennesaw was not so much on account of its inapproachable, perpendicular sides, but by its being the best watch-tower ever possessed by an army. Before the eye of the rebel signal officer, on the highest point of Kennesaw, Sherman's army lay fully exposed. Not a movement of a regiment in daylight that could not be detected and due notice given. And, if changes were made during the cover of darkness, the succeeding day discovered them all to that all-seeing eye.

The rebel line, as before stated, was first fixed about a mile in front of Kennesaw, on some high grounds that ran along parallel with that mountain. On the 15th, the 81st Ohio moved out of bivouac, for the purpose of supporting a portion of the Corps which was making an advance. The regiment did not, however, go into action. The movement of the day resulted successfully to the Union army—a large number of prisoners being captured. General Veatch's Division, in this movement, formed the advance of the 16th Corps, Colonel Sprague's Brigade forming the with the naked eye, they could see where our shell burst, and where the solid shot tore up the earth and threw the dust about the rebel works. Every good shot was vehemently cheered, and the artillery practice became a regular source of amusement.

The 27th of June was a bloody day before Kennesaw, although, as before stated, not much was done in front of the 16th Corps. It was at the close of this exciting day, when, at a battery whose guns had just ceased their booming and roaring at the mountain, there arose in sweetest melody the sound of music. It was a quartette of male voices, and the song was—"We'll be gay and happy still." Very fitting, it seemed to be, to hear under those guns, the ringing chorus—

> "Then let the cannon boom as they will,
> We'll be gay and happy still!"

The singers were adepts. Their voices were clear and strong, the evening air was calm and still, and as the sound of their song floated over the neighboring camps, the weary soldiers crept instinctively toward the singers, to luxuriate in the harmony of "sweet song." The singers had no grand house made with hands, where, amid the glare of gas-light, giving back the flash of costly diamonds, and the more potent sparkling of beauty's witching eyes, the listeners could languish in luxurious ease. But such an audience never experienced rarer or truer delight than did these soldiers, stretched on the bare earth, beneath the green roof of "God's first temples," and listening to the familiar airs of "Vacant chair," and "Home again;" while, in fancy, they heard, far away, the same songs sung in softer tones, as they used to delight to hear them, when home was not a myth. Far into the night the "concert" continued, while the sharp staccato of the skirmisher's rifle on the mountain side, bore a suggestive accompaniment.

advance of the Division. Their skirmishers, on the 15th, were obliged to move through an open field on the enemy's works. I say works, because the rebel skirmishers had made quite strong defenses, by throwing together, with close intervals, piles of rails, and covering them with earth.

During the night following this advance, our pioneers and pickets worked almost together. The pioneers, with pick and shovel, silently throwing out the loose red earth, to form defenses, while the pickets protected them in their labor. The supporting lines also threw up earthworks in the rear, close behind the advanced lines. An almost level valley, half a mile in width, and extending indefinitely in length, contained all of the 15th and 16th Corps. On the southern side of the valley, just on the border of the woods, in plain view of all the supporting troops, our picket line was established. In the morning our pickets discovered the rebel picket line intrenched from fifty to two hundred yards in their front. In this position our lines remained until the 19th of June. All day the pickets' guns were continually popping, the artillery was trying its power, while the reserves were kept closely to arms, ready for any emergency. The rebels were exceedingly careful of their artillery ammunition. It was even amusing, tragical as it must have been, to witness the firing of the rebel artillery, and our own. There were one or two rebel batteries situated on a bluff bank, in front of the 15th Corps, and in plain view of the 81st Ohio. Now and then we could see the curling, white smoke from one of their guns, and could hear the hearty cheer with which Logan's war-worn heroes greeted the sound of the rebel shell, flying over their heads. Our own artillery was generally silent until the rebels had ventured two or three shots, and then, having thrown them off their guard somewhat, a whole battery of Logan's Parrotts would hurl its hissing shell plump into the rebel battery, effectually silencing them for the next hour or more. On our right, in front of the 14th Corps, during these days, there was a very lively cannonading, out of our sight, but in hearing. One battery in that Corps, which we only knew by the sobriquet of "old leather breeches," used to bring a cheer from the whole Union line by its odd mode of firing. All its guns were charged at once, and each one was properly sighted, and then, at a given signal, they were discharged so nearly together that it was almost impossible to tell whether it was the report of one great gun or six ordinary ones.

While the armies lay in this position there was but little opportunity for any thing like rest, even to those not immediately in the front, or on duty. The reserves were so near the enemy's skirmish line, that frequently their balls fell behind our defenses, and the only safety was in lying close behind the works. Even then, it was almost impossible to get a whole night's rest, for, every few hours, a violent skirmish firing somewhere along the line, would suggest another night attack, and, without waiting for the formality of a command, the whole line of reserves would tumble out of their bivouac beds, and, fully armed and equipped, would almost intuitively take their places at the works, and wait until the excitement subsided. Nor could they ever become so accustomed to these little half alarms, so as to become careless. *Semper paratus* was the practical watchword of each soldier.

The men were virtually imprisoned behind their own defenses, and the only relief which they had was at night, when a new "relief" went on duty, and were disposed to make their night's work as agreeable as possible. This was done by some one calling out—"Say, Johnny reb., don't you want to rest awhile? We'll not shoot if you wont." The terms were usually gladly accepted, and a temporary truce was thus established. The fact that these arrangements were always made by the men, and not by the officers, made it certain that no advantage would be taken to change position, or any thing of that kind, during the continuance of the truce. The truth was, that both armies were so tired out by the continual excitement of alarms, that men were willing to get what rest they could in any way. After a few moments of quiet, natural inquisitiveness, or a love of adventure, would lead some one to propound some question to the opposite party, in general. Whoever could first answer, or whoever chose, could be the spokesman of his side. In this way amusing conversations were often carried on, always in the best spirit.

One night, in front of the 15th Corps, during one of these truces, a general conversation had taken place, and the men of both sides had advanced in front of their respective lines, disarmed, of course, until they were nearly together. Attracted by the novelty of the sight, great numbers of troops from the main line had also gone out to see the fun. Some one of the rebels asked for a song, and a choir of singers among our soldiers responded in clear, manly tones, under the soft moonlight, with the suggestive air of "Just before the battle, Mother." When this was ended, the rebels cheered heartily in applause, and declared that the new song was an excellent one. They then returned the compliment by singing one for us, which our boys, in turn applauded. Then a proposition to exchange papers was made, and was carried into effect, but just as the parties who had met half way, had separated, some one, rebel or Union, we could not tell, who was away to the right, and who knew nothing of the arrangement, fired. Instantly, at the same place, a picket volley answered, and the trucers, each supposing that the opposite party was getting treacherous, took to their heels and gained their respective works, inwardly execrating the wretch who broke the truce by firing the unlucky shot.

True to their word, not a shot was fired along the neutral portion of the line until every man of both sides had got safely behind the defenses. But then, the men who, but a minute before, had engaged in friendly conversation and song, began their work of death again; threw off the white robe of Peace, and assumed the red mantle of War.

This was the history of almost every night of these four or five days, of what may be characterized as the siege of the approaches to Kennesaw Mountain. The 81st Ohio took but a passive part, until midnight of the 16th, when it moved to the support of Colonel Sprague's Brigade, whose widening front left it bare of reserves. Although the distance to march that night was scarcely more than a mile, yet the remainder of the night was spent on the way, through some blunder of somebody—that mysterious person who never can be named or known in military affairs. The next day one battalion of the regiment moved to the front, and built intrenchments near where the railroad passed through our lines. That portion of the regiment remained there until the 19th. Before daylight of the 19th, the remaining battalion went out on duty on the picket line in front of Colonel Sprague's Brigade. The relieving was done with the utmost care, as the rebel line was but a hundred yards or so in front of the Union intrenchments, and to expose the person above the works, was to devote that soldier to almost certain death. As daylight came on, the rebel skirmish fire seemed to be wanting. Was it a cruel ruse to get our men to raise their heads and receive a fatal shot? Yankee inquisitiveness was not to be suppressed by this possibility. Here and there some soldier ventured toward the rebel defenses, and found them deserted. It took an hour or two to report this fact, and receive orders, but at the end of that time the whole skirmish line advanced cautiously. General Sherman, with his usual nervous style, telegraphed the War Department that the rebels had retreated, and he was going to start in a few minutes for Marietta. It is said that he gave orders for one or two trains to move into Marietta.

The skirmishers of the 16th Corps, resting their right on the railroad, advanced. After passing the enemy's works there was, in front, an almost unbroken forest. Passing through this in a heavy rain, now halting, now going to the left, now to the right, now forward, never certain where we were going, or when we would stop, it was a positive relief when, at about three o'clock in the afternoon, the rattling of Confederate bullets among the trees over our heads, told that the enemy had not gone entirely away. The skirmish line having orders to move on until the enemy was found, now halted, literally at the base of Kennesaw Mountain. General Sherman, discovered now that the way to Marietta lay over that mountain. In the evening, soon after we had found the enemy, a locomotive was sent forward to see how far it could proceed. It came to a building which was well supplied with wood, all ready for use, wooded up, and, finding it was almost up with our skirmish line, concluded to retire. Uttering a shrill whistle as it started, it was discovered by the rebels, and, bang! bang! went two pieces of artillery from the summit of Kennesaw, after the retreating engine. The engineer made excellent time to the rear, escaping unhurt, but determining to find wood elsewhere after that treatment.

The rebels had made the summit of the mountain their new line, and had planted several pieces of artillery there. Large details were also at work on the mountain side near the top, apparently making rifle pits there. Those of us who waded through that day's varying skirmishing experience, in the woods and rain, had anything but a comfortable prospect for the night, as we watched those dirty men almost directly above us, and imagined that we could see them engaged in the amiable business of detaching huge rocks, which, in the stillness of the night, they would send whirling down on our devoted heads! It was something of a compensation, and was even a sublime pleasure, to see, as we did, the hasty dropping of tools, on the part of these piously intentioned rebels, and hurried rushing behind trees and rocks, as one of our whizzing shells, from a battery far in our rear, would burst among the rocks and crags of the mountain. We heard no sweeter music that day, than the dull thud of that battery, and the sharp whistle of its shells flying over our heads.

Kennesaw Mountain! What soldier who saw it during these days, will ever forget its fiery-flaming brow? Into how many households does the name bring the gushing tears of sorrow for the loved one whose spark of life went out before that death-dealing giant of Nature? Kennesaw Mountain held Sherman's army at bay fourteen days, during which the loss in killed and wounded was greater than at any previous part of the campaign. Very fortunately, the 81st Ohio, though almost all of that time in the front line, and often on picket duty, yet was not called to make an assault at any time. On the 27th, a portion of the regiment went out under Lieutenant-Colonel Adams, in support of a charging column of the 16th Corps; but as the grand attack along the whole line was so disastrously repulsed that day, on the right, and the physical impossibility of proceeding in front of the 16th Corps, prevented any serious advance in that part of the line, the battalion met with no loss.

CHAPTER XII.

ATLANTA CAMPAIGN—FROM KENNESAW MOUNTAIN TO NEAR ATLANTA.

Probably never before did so large a number of spectators have the privilege of witnessing so grand a spectacle of artillery practice as occurred while we lay before Kennesaw. The rebels had about twelve guns on the left, or western part of the mountain—three or four more near the center, and half a dozen at the right, or eastern part. On these guns the Union army could certainly bring to bear fifty—perhaps more, for there were at least the 17th, 16th, 15th and 14th Corps whose guns were in range. The summit of Kennesaw was so sharply defined against the sky, and the brow so shorn of trees, that every man who appeared about a gun could be seen by our whole line. On the other hand, the rebels, from their elevated position, had a perfect bird's-eye view of our entire operations. Under such circumstances, it may be imagined that the artillery combats would be frequent and exciting. For the first two or three days the rebels were very chary of their guns, not replying sometimes for hours to our almost constant cannonade. During these days they were only getting ready, building traverses and bomb-proofs for the safety of their gunners. They also made their works for the protection of their guns, as perfect as possible. On the third or fourth day, however, about eight o'clock in the morning, as our gunners leisurely began their customary popping, the whole army was aroused by a fast and furious cannonading from the western battery on Kennesaw. Hardly was the first volley given until one after another, the rebel guns in quick succession belched forth a second offering. By this time the whole army, along

McPherson's lines, was in line—not to fight—but to look. The rebel shell and shot always passed over the infantry, which was too close to the mountain to allow the depression of the guns sufficiently to do any harm. It was, therefore, perfectly safe to stand out and see the fight. And so vigorously did the rebels ply their guns, that our bewildered artillerists seemed enchained by the extraordinary sight, and were very slow to send back an answering shot. Perceiving this, the rebels, who had lain closely behind their works, began to boldly come out, until, between the eyes of our soldiers and the sky beyond, the dirty figures of the exultant rebels thickly covered the crest of the mountain. As the fight progressed, and our guns still were silent, these dirty legions sent up shout after shout of defiance, while the Union soldiers could only look silently on, and wonder why our batteries were still. At last our gunners seemed to recover their self-possession, and the first shell thrown fell close to a rebel gun, but not until the swarming line of rebel heads which "had marked its coming," but did not "grow brighter when it came," had securely hid themselves behind their fortifications. Then, as thick and fast fell the well-aimed shells from our batteries, among the smoke and flash of the rebel guns, it was our time to cheer. Growing excited in the contest, every gun of ours that could reach the rebel line, and many that could not, opened upon them. The rebels held out manfully for awhile, but as one after another of our batteries opened on them, in front and flank, they were at last compelled to lie still, or only fire when a lull of a minute gave them opportunity. It was a grand scene. The Union troops could distinctly see the rebel guns fire, and could hear the flight of their shell, and their angry bursting far overhead, but could not see the effect of any that fell among our batteries, they being mostly in rear of the infantry lines. But with glasses, and even

After the disastrous termination of the assault on the 27th of June, General Sherman, seeing that the position could not be stormed without too great loss of life, set his brain to work to devise other means. As usual, he decided on another flanking expedition, and, as usual, also, he appointed the gallant McPherson to lead the way. The maturing of his plan, and the preparation for its execution, occupied several days. On the 2d of July, the movement of wagon trains of McPherson's command, away to the right, was completed, and that night the left of the army withdrew and began its movement in the same direction. The 17th Corps moved first—the 16th following. The night was extremely dark, and a number of mistakes occurred to cause portions of the column to take the wrong roads, and thus delay the movement, so that just before daylight the 81st Ohio went into bivouac, scarcely two miles from where it started. From a brief sleep the soldiers were early aroused by the news that the Stars and Stripes were flying on Kennesaw! True enough, while we, with the utmost silence and secresy, were escaping from the rebels, they were just as cautiously running away from us. They did not entirely leave Marietta until after daylight, when a train of cars left with the rails from a portion of the railroad track, which was torn up to prevent General Sherman from riding into Marietta in triumph. Notwithstanding the evacuation of Kennesaw and Marietta, the movement of McPherson's army was continued, with but slight modifications. On the night of the 3d, the 16th Corps had passed beyond the positions of the Army of the Cumberland and of the Ohio. One Brigade (2d of 2d Division) crossing Nickajack Creek at Ruff's Mills, relieved a Brigade of the 15th Corps, which, during the afternoon, had been engaged with the enemy at that place. The Brigade did not reach its position until after dark, and then throwing out skirmishers a short distance in advance, bivouacked in line of battle. In the morning, the 4th Division, General Veatch, crossed the creek and passed out a short distance and formed in line of battle. In this way it advanced, until it found the enemy strongly posted, only a half mile or so from where Colonel Mersey's Brigade had bivouacked that night. The Second Division was soon ordered up to take position on the right of the 4th. About noon, while the 81st Ohio was advancing toward the front, passing through a lane in rear of the line of the 4th Division, Lieutenant Lockwood received a severe wound from a rebel ball striking his leg. A member of Company I, about the same time had a hole cut through his hat, and his ear grazed by another ball. It was evident that we were again coming in contact with the enemy whom we had hoped to not see again on this side of the Chattahoochee. Without further loss, the 81st Ohio formed in line on the right of the 66th Illinois, which joined the 39th Ohio, of the 4th Division. The 12th Illinois was formed close in rear, in reserve, and the First Brigade was placed still further on the right. Earthworks were immediately thrown up, as, by this time, the wagons containing intrenching tools had become quite as favored as Headquarters' teams, and were always kept close at the heels of each Brigade. It was not long after noon, and intensely hot, when the brave boys of the 81st Ohio celebrated the Fourth of July by digging vigorously into the red soil of the Southern Confederacy in the State of Georgia. They had a picnic dinner, too, in the woods, of most simple and frugal kind. Hard tack and salt pork with coffee, and no other dessert, formed the staples of the feast. There was no music; but the burning of powder, and the big noise consequent, was more extensive than agreeable. Neither were there any speeches of the usual spread eagle character, but the Flag was there, and, in the soft rustle of its silken folds, as it floated to the breeze in that Georgian forest, it aroused more of patriotism in the hearts of those who were proud to have borne it thus far in honor, than would have been awakened by a hundred speeches. And so we worked on, glad that we were allowed the privilege of thus celebrating the day, though not unmindful of the fact that it were infinitely easier to celebrate it far more ostentatiously and grandly away up North, out of hearing of war, than it was here.

Soon the 66th Illinois was called out to strengthen the skirmish line, and it connected with the skirmishers of the 39th Ohio. About three o'clock, all things were ready for a charge on the enemy's works! It was to be made by the 4th Division—the skirmishers of the 2d Division to co-operate. In front of the latter, at but a short distance, the enemy had, in an open field, a strongly intrenched picket line, which was farther protected by the felling of the underbrush at the edge of the woods through which our troops must pass to reach the works, in such a manner as to delay them in easy range of the rebel guns. It was any thing but a desirable piece of work with which to close a celebration of the Fourth of July, but in this case the programme had to be strictly followed. With rare gallantry, the 39th and 27th Ohio regiments moved through an open field, resistlessly onward against the enemy's intrenched line, and, of course, took it. At nearly the same time the 66th Illinois took up the shout, and springing from behind their cover, rushed down upon the enemy's intrenched skirmish line, and took it, with a number of prisoners. On the right of the 66th, the 2d Iowa captured other works and prisoners.

It was now nearly sunset. It was evident that the rebels were in full force, and as we had gained ground, it was thought necessary to intrench, in order to hold it. Accordingly, the 66th Illinois was gathered toward the left, and the 12th Illinois, 52d Illinois and 66th Indiana were placed on its right, and set to work at converting the rebel works into solid Union intrenchments. After sunset the rebels shelled our working parties pretty severely, causing some injury. About one o'clock that night, an order came for the 81st Ohio to relieve the 66th Illinois, and complete the work it had begun. From their beds on the hard earth, the men reluctantly arose, and, in the pitchy darkness, the regiment silently started toward its destination, moving by the flank, in two ranks. It was a dense woods where they had been lying, and there was no path to follow. Moving along the sleeping lines, the head of the column at last crossed the earthworks, and found a road leading to the front. On this, Colonel Adams led his command to their destination, and was just about to assign the different companies to their positions, when he discovered that but two or three companies were present. Nobody could tell where the others were, and so a search was instituted. Going back toward the place of starting, he met the rest on the way. The night was so dark, and the way so crooked, that there had been a gap in the line before the regiment crossed the works, and the leader of the hindmost battalion, thus formed, lost sight of his file leader, and missed his way. It was nearly daylight when the regiment got into position, and then the poor men, exhausted and sleepy as they were, had to dig once more, to complete the half finished works.

When daylight came, our skirmishers reported no enemy in front. The rebels had again fallen back, and we had the poor satisfaction of knowing that while we were losing sleep and digging earth, the enemy was also losing sleep, but instead of planning to attack us, as we thought, he was making all possible speed to escape. The regiment rested until 1 P. M.—enjoying in the meantime as only soldiers can enjoy, the luxury of a full mail bringing letters and papers from home. By sunset the 81st Ohio was in bivouac at Widow Gordon's or Mitchell's on the Sandtown road, about four miles from the Chattahoochee river. Here, during the 6th and 7th, the regiment rested, taking such comfort as could be had in a little hot field, enclosed on two sides by a woods which, while it cast no welcome shadow, kept the wind from reaching us from those sides. Still it was made to contribute innumerable boughs of oak and pine, whose leafy limbs were made to keep out the sunshine from the little tenements which the men always built wherever they slept.

The enemy at this time had commenced crossing the Chattahoochee, and for this purpose had concentrated his forces nearer the railroad. McPherson's army was now at the extreme right of the army, and close to the river. Early on the morning of the 8th, the 81st Ohio, with the rest of the Brigade, was ordered forward and advanced nearly to the river. There the 81st was detached and sent to relieve the 66th Illinois, which had been on picket on the river bank. The left of the line was almost on the bank at Baker's Ferry, while toward the right, the line ran along some high ground, along a fence, some three or four hundred yards from the river. Companies C and I were posted behind a little bank near the Ferry, with orders to keep up a sharp firing, as if attempting to effect a crossing. A few men crept cautiously down toward the Ferry, where an outpost was established, and where, by exercising great care, a shot at very close range could occasionally be given. So the day passed; while one relief was firing, the rest were lying in the shade, or luxuriating upon the ripe blackberries which grew there so abundantly. Toward evening, a peremptory command came to cease firing, and the boys were glad enough to hear it, as scarcely one was not afflicted by that time with a sore shoulder from the recoil of the gun.

Among those who manifested bravery of the highest

degree, that day, and whose name may be mentioned here without disparagement to any of the others—for he is dead—is Private Fletcher B. Haynes, of Company C. At the beginning of the campaign he was not on duty with the Company, being Regimental Armorer. But, as, during the march he could do nothing in that capacity, he voluntarily assumed his place in the ranks, and carried his gun—a revolving carbine, into whatever action the Company went. Being an excellent marksman, he went that day to the out-post before mentioned, and ascertaining during the day that a point blank range upon the rebel battery could be obtained at a little distance from the defense which screened the party, he conceived the idea of building a barricade at that point, as soon as darkness should render it practicable. When darkness came, he went to work, and by occasionally ducking low to the ground, as a careless rebel sent a bullet over his head, he succeeded in getting a perfect defense built, from which, when daylight came, he could try his gun against the rebel cannon. Morning came, and when the rebel gunners made their appearance to pay their respects to our artillery, a bang! from Haynes' gun sent a ball plump through the embrasure, and the cannon was not loaded. Again they essayed it, but another ball from his unerring gun drove them away, and thus, from daylight until he was relieved, he effectually silenced that twelve pounder with his little carbine.

About seven o'clock, on the morning of the ninth of July, the pickets were withdrawn, and almost immediately the march was commenced toward Marietta. Another flank movement was to be made, and for the fifth time in this campaign, McPherson was deputed to make the movement. He had, by his demonstrations along the river, on the right, drawn the attention of the rebels in that direction, and now, although it was at the hight of the heat of a Georgian July, it was thought necessary to move his whole army from the extreme right to the extreme left. It may have been best, but it seemed then that troops nearer the left would have made the movement with far less trouble. However, it is not for soldiers to

"——question why,
Their's but to do and die."

This time the 16th Corps had the advance, and with a fatality which seemed always to attend the movement of an army, there was a harassing delay which made it afternoon when the 81st Ohio started. It was eighteen miles to Marietta, which place was to be the end of that day's march. As a matter of course, taking into account the inevitable delays on account of stoppages of the artillery and wagon trains, it was after midnight when the 81st went into bivouac, tired and worn out with the continual watching and marching which had been the portion of a part of the regiment for the previous forty hours.

During this night march there was a curious occurrence which I will here record for the benefit of students of the science of mind. The regiment was marching by flank in the usual way, and had just passed through one of the rebel lines of works around Marietta, when suddenly there was a rushing sound heard by those in the rear from toward the front of the regiment, accompanied by cries of "Look out!" "Hi! Hi!" "Get out of the way!" "Take care!" The sound and rush seemed to begin at the head of the regiment and to move rapidly toward the rear. I was near the rear and to me it was so sudden that I had no time to reflect until I found myself running with all possible speed, with every body else, out of the road. Apparently something—no one could tell what—runned down the road through the dividing ranks, with the speed of a locomotive; and so vivid was the impression on most of the troops, that something had passed, that there was quite a lively discussion, for a time, as to whether it was a squad of rebel cavalry, a runaway horse, or some Government cattle on a stampede. As there were large herds of cattle near by, the latter supposition had most supporters. But nobody could be found who had seen any thing; they had only heard something going at mad speed through the regiment, and then the sound ceased. It was dark, yet a horse or steer could have been seen. What was it? Really it was nothing more material than a panic in its purest and most ethereal form. A mule, at the woodside, in its death struggles, rattled some bushes and frightened the horses of the officers at the head of the column. As these backed a little toward the men, the ranks opened on either side of the road, and some one indiscreetly cried out, "look out!" So accustomed were the men to do just as their file leaders did, that one after another, they separated the whole length of the regiment, as before stated, without knowing why. At what particular point, and why, the idea of something passing arose, I can not tell. The matter was a subject of both wonder and merriment for a long time.

Very early on the morning of the 10th of July the regiment was *en route* for Roswell, a manufacturing town on the Chattahoochee, about twelve or fourteen miles from Marietta. We reached it at 1 P. M., having so exhausted the troops by the ascent of a long hill, totally unprotected by shade, that on reaching the summit where there was a woods and shade, our regiment numbered less than eighty men in ranks! Nor were other regiments any better. And those who by their iron will did keep in their places, were so nearly exhausted that they, too, would have succumbed in a few minutes more if a halt had not been made. Men fell out of ranks then, who had never done so before. I think we never passed through so severe an ordeal in marching.

We spent the rest of the afternoon in crossing the river, to relieve Newton's Division of the 4th Corps. The crossing was effected without the use of bridge or pontoons—the men waded across! The stream was but about twenty inches deep at the place where we crossed, but it was at least three hundred yards wide, and the current was quite strong. The Brigade commanded by Colonel Sprague, crossed in some style—marching with two regiments side by side, companies in line, and preceded by a brass band, discoursing music all the sweeter for being on the water.

As usual, before the almost exhausted troops lay down to rest and sleep, they built a line of intrenchments, such as in other times they would have required a day to complete. But this situation had one charm for our ears: we could sleep at night without hearing the skirmishers' everlasting bang! bang! at the front. We could only hear in the distance, toward the right, the heavy boom of the far off cannon, with which we had no concern. The men actually rested here. With a forest in which to bivouac, protected from the heat of the sun, a river to bathe in, and numerous springs of sparkling water to quench thirst, there was real comfort in the situation.

Here we lay until the morning of the 16th of July, by which time the remainder of McPherson's army had arrived. General Dodge, with his characteristic energy, had rebuilt the long bridge over the Chattahoochee, so that wagons passed over it on the morning of the 14th—being hardly three days' work. The bridge was a substantial structure, made of what lumber could be found at the mills, eked out by the flooring of many of the buildings of Roswell.

Johnston now found that Sherman had a fixed lodgment on the Atlanta side of the river, and that his communications were again in danger; he therefore withdrew to that side with all his army, and Sherman followed. Using the right as a pivot, Sherman moved his line like the hand of a clock, resistlessly onward, pushing every thing before it. Starting on the 16th, the 15th and 16th Corps, on parallel roads, had the advance of McPherson's army. The movement was nearly southward, and was made to the extent of about ten miles with but little opposition. Late in the afternoon, the 9th Illinois (mounted,) had a lively skirmish with rebel cavalry, losing several men. And as the infantry came up, there was a brisk little fight, between a battery or two of ours, and one of the enemy's. Lieutenant Laird, 14th Ohio Battery, got two or three of his guns in position, and with such unerring precision did he send his shot and shell that we could see the rebels hastily evacuating their temporary position, and making all possible speed toward the rear. General McPherson and General Dodge were much at the front, even when the rebel shell were flying thickly there. There was no movement of that army which was not seen and known personally by the almost omnipresent McPherson. Where there was to be danger or difficulty, he seemed instinctively to know it, and he was invariably present to give his valuable aid.

The next day the movement was continued, with slight skirmishing, during the day. The troops were encamped that night in line, near Nancy's Creek. The next day, the 18th of July, an advance was made with almost constant skirmishing, to Peach Tree Creek, and on the 19th, the Army of the Tennessee reached Decatur. General Schofield's troops had a sharp little contest at the edge of the town, but as General Logan's troops, and the advance of General Dodge's, were coming in at the other side, the rebels retired. Schofield's troops were moved a little to the right, so as to leave the town to General McPherson's command. General Dodge's Corps occupied that portion of the town nearest Atlanta, and was very unexpectedly saluted by a rebel battery, just about sunset, as General

Fuller's Division was going into position for the night. The shell struck his column, and created a considerable disturbance in the bivouac of the men and mules of the 9th Illinois. This command hastily sought a more secluded camp for the night. General Fuller's troops took refuge in lying flat down, while he hurried up his famous 14th Ohio Battery, which, in a very short time, drove the rebels from their position, and allowed us to rest during the remainder of the night in peace.

On the 20th of July, the Army of the Cumberland, which formed the right of the whole army, fought the bloody battle of Peach Tree Creek; while we lay peaceably in bivouac at Decatur. Some idea of the vastness of Sherman's operations may be had from the fact that McPherson's army did not know that Thomas had been fighting. The artillery was heard, of course, but that was of so frequent occurrence that it was scarcely observed at all.

With the successful termination of that battle, our lines began to close in around Atlanta. On the 21st of July, the 17th Corps took position on the extreme left, having a fierce battle for the possession of a commanding eminence, called by the army, Bald Hill. The 15th Corps joined it on the right, and the 16th was mostly left in reserve. General Sweeney's Division was placed in line with the 15th, one Brigade of General Fuller's Division in rear of the 17th Corps and Colonel Sprague's Brigade left in charge of Decatur. Formidable lines of earthworks protected the long line of our army from McPherson's left to Thomas' right. The usual amount of skirmishing and artillery practice had been in progress all day. Night settled on the two armies, lying in close array, entirely oblivious of the grand and bloody scene that was to be enacted on the morrow.

CHAPTER XIII.

ATLANTA CAMPAIGN—BATTLES OF JULY 22D AND 28TH.

The morning of the 22d of July shone brightly on the Union Army, awakened early with the news that Atlanta was in our possession. Skirmishers were sent forward, who found the half-finished works of the rebels deserted, but before the city itself was reached, it was discovered that the enemy had but withdrawn to their inner stronghold. General Johnston had been superseded by Hood, and this ambitious fighting general was making his first brilliant maneuver. He had withdrawn to his inner lines for the purpose of sending an overwhelming force around our left, to attack us in flank and rear. A mere accident saved us from even the headlong tactics of this most unfortunate general.

Early in the morning, orders had been given to push forward the whole line to that lately occupied by the rebels, and intrench there. General Sweeney's Division had been ordered from its position with the 15th Corps, and with the Brigade of General Fuller's Division, in rear of the 17th Corps, was to take position on the left of the 17th Corps, so soon as it should get its line established. As soon as the order was given, General Dodge went to the ground designated, and made a thorough view of it, previous to assigning his troops to their places. The 17th Corps, not getting its new line established very rapidly, General Sweeney's Division, on reaching a point in rear of the Brigade of General Fuller's Division, halted to await orders. As the troops then were, General Dodge's command was lying nearly a half mile in rear of the center of the line of the 17th Corps. It was twelve o'clock, when some stray skirmish shots were heard in the woods, near

General Sweeney's Division. In a few minutes, a staff officer rode up to General Dodge, (who had just returned from the front, and was eating dinner with General Fuller) and told him of the firing, and said that there seemed to be a body of rebels there. As this was so very far in rear of the 17th Corps, it seemed incredible that a force should have passed their flank, nevertheless, General Dodge sent an order to General Sweeney to put his command in line of battle, and telling General Fuller to have his command under arms immediately, he mounted, and rode over to where General Sweeney was. It was an open field, bounded on the south by a wide belt of forest. A little ridge ran southwardly through the field toward the forest. To the right of it, ran a stream, in the same direction, toward which the ground on either side gently declined. General Sweeney's Division was posted with the right resting near this stream, extending up to the ridge, where nearly all the artillery was placed, then bending back at right angles and running along the ridge. The right regiment was the 12th Illinois, and immediately on its left was the 81st Ohio, (three companies of which were in reserve under Captain Hill,) which extended as far as to the artillery. General Fuller placed his Brigade on the west side of the stream mentioned, in a line nearly in continuation of the right of General Sweeney's. Hardly were these dispositions made, until the artillery at the angle of General Sweeney's line was suddenly and fiercely assaulted by a strong column of rebels, emerging almost without notice, from the woods so near in front. Belching forth their quick volleys of canister, full in the faces of the foe, it seemed that the guns of Blodgett and Laird (the former Company H, 1st Missouri Light Artillery, and the latter, 14th Ohio Battery) would alone be invincible; but the determination of the rebels was great, and their rashness such as only Hood could inspire. Their numbers, we soon saw, were not to be despised Pouring out of the woods on the right and left, almost enveloping the three Brigades which formed the 16th Corps, it looked as if there could be no escape from defeat and surrender. At one time the Brigade of Colonel Morrill, (General Fuller's Division,) was forced back, temporarily by a deadly flank fire poured upon it from a line in the woods on its right, but nobly rallying, and partially changing front, it advanced again to victory.

General Sweeney's command stood like a rock. Never was there more daring or more effective resistance made, than by both his infantry and artillery; attacked as they were with scarcely a moment's warning, and without the slightest defenses. At an opportune moment, Captain Hill's reserve, ordered forward by General Dodge, took position in a gap between the 81st Ohio and 12th Illinois, and these regiments moved forward in a grand triumphal charge, carrying every thing before them and driving the dismayed foe in terror from the field. The 81st Ohio, in this charge, captured a number of prisoners and three rebel battle flags. With this, the rebels were apparently satisfied to yield the contest. They had marched nearly all the previous night, and had expected to take us completely by surprise, as they would have done, if it had not been for the mere accidental position of General Sweeney's Division. Finding this force in the very place they had expected to find nothing, and meeting with such determined and destructive resistance, they became heartily discouraged, and fell back under cover of the woods.

In the meantime, other rebel columns had been at work elsewhere. The first attack was made on General Dodge, but the rest followed quickly. One column gained the immediate rear of the 17th Corps, and crushing it, the column swept along in rear undisturbed, until they reached a little road on which General McPherson was riding, alone, toward the line of the 17th Corps, all ignorant of the presence of an enemy in the rear of his command. At that point, the General was suddenly confronted by a line of rebels. There was no order to halt, no demand for surrender, but a volley of musketry crashed through the woods, and the gallant and beloved McPherson was stretched on the ground. His horse escaping unhurt, ran into our lines and was the first to carry the sad news of his rider's death. On the same road, about the same time, another portion of this rebel line came suddenly upon the battery of Lieutenant Murray, ("F" 2d U. S. Artillery,) which was at the time passing from the line of the 17th Corps to General Fuller. The horses were shot down, and the guns and men captured. Still further to the right the rebel line struck the works of the 17th Corps in flank, and drove the men of that Corps back slowly toward Bald Hill, where the right of the Corps rested. These men were not driven by fear. Fighting desperately now from one side and then from the other of their works, they only went back as they found themselves nearly cut off from the rest of the army.

A half mile or more to the right, another rebel column made a direct assault on the line held by the 15th Corps, near the railroad. Rushing through a railroad cut, which, apparently, was not defended, the rebels gained a flank fire on our troops, and forced them to retire, leaving the guns of the celebrated DeGres' Battery in the enemy's hands. This was late in the afternoon. General Dodge's troops had driven away their assailants, and were busy in erecting defenses against another assault. General Logan had been assigned to the command made vacant by the death of McPherson. In the emergency of the partial repulse of the 15th Corps, he called on General Dodge for a Brigade to aid in retrieving the lost works. Colonel Mersey's Brigade was sent. By the road which they had to march, the distance was nearly two miles, yet these men, who had already fought a desperate and exhaustive battle, and who had afterward been hard at work in building works, moved at double quick most of the way, and immediately joined in a charge by which the line which had been lost was recovered, and the guns retaken. A detail from the 81st Ohio assisted Captain DeGres in serving his guns upon the retreating rebels. So zealous were they in this work that one of the guns burst from the effects of its heavy charges.

So ended the battle, with the exception of a most bloody and persistent attack on the small portion of the 17th Corps, crowded together on Bald Hill. Night put a stop to the desperate hand to hand conflict, which raged there nearly all the afternoon.

To show the intensity of the struggle in General Dodge's front, it may be stated that Lieutenant Blodgett's Battery fired over four hundred rounds, mostly case and canister; while that of Lieutenant Laird fired over six hundred rounds of the same kind. On this little front our troops buried one hundred and fifty dead rebels, after the battle. Many more were carried off and buried by the enemy. The ordnance officer of one Division reported having picked up 1,200 guns, abandoned by the enemy. General Dodge's command took prisoners representing forty-nine different regiments.

Among those who fell to rise no more in the first victorious charge made by the 81st Ohio, was Captain Charles Lane, commanding Company K. A rebel bullet pierced his head, and his death was instantaneous. To say that he died at his post in defense of his country, gives him an immortality of honor on the bright roll of his country's heroes; to say that he was beloved by his men, and respected by his fellow officers; that he was one of the very few in the army possessing firmness sufficient to resist its temptations; that his private character was stainless; that his example was that of a noble Christian soldier—all this may render his memory dear to his friends, and reconcile them in part to his loss. But around his widowed and orphaned hearthstone are lonely hearts gathered to whom no eulogy can bring the balm of consolation. Theirs is a grief too sacred and tender for human touch.

Upon the death of Captain Lane, Lieutenant Hezekiah Hoover succeeded to the command of the Company. He led it to the assault subsequently made by the Brigade upon the line of works lost by the 15th Corps, and there, while advancing, was struck by a piece of shell and instantly killed. Thus, within a few hours, two officers of the same company fell to rise no more. Their bodies were tenderly borne by their bereaved comrades to their last resting place, and decently interred.

Late in the night of the 22d, the tired soldiers of Colonel Mersey's Brigade were awakened and moved over to Bald Hill. This was in consequence of the importance of the position, and of the fact that the soldiers who were occupying it were exhausted, and were so mixed up that their commanders were unwilling to depend on them in case of a determined night assault. It was a compliment to the bravery of this Brigade to be assigned to this important position, but the boys did not so understand it, and they only thought they were being overworked. The rebels never renewed the attack; they had lost terribly in killed and wounded, amounting to over seven thousand, while our loss was but three thousand five hundred. Still, our troops, taking lessons in building defenses from the new mode of attack to which they had been subjected, built such works as they never had built before. On Bald Hill, the 12th Illinois and 81st Ohio had a perfect labyrinth of works. They had no flanks, no rear! These they peaceably occupied during the succeeding three or four days, annoyed only by an occasional skirmisher's shot.

During these days of rest after the battle of the 22d, the term of service of Colonel Mersey expired, and that officer, so long in command of the Brigade, to which the 81st Ohio belonged, took his leave of his soldiers. As he passed through the command with which he had been so long connected, his feelings overpowered him, and tears, instead of words, told of the strong attachment with which he was bound to them. It was a touching parting scene, on that hot and bloody battle field. The Colonel received a highly complimentary letter upon the occasion of his departure from General Dodge, as an extract will show:

"You leave at a time and under circumstances of which you and your command may justly be proud. Fighting as you did, on three different fields the same day, and victorious on every one, forms the best and most honorable reward that you can take with you. I again heartily thank you for all you have done, and trust that you will not forget old associates in any new field you may choose.

I am, very respectfully,
G. M. DODGE,
Major General."

This left Lieutenant-Colonel Phillips, of the 9th Illinois, in command of the Brigade. About the same time, General Sweeney, commanding the Division, was arrested and ordered to Nashville for trial, upon charges preferred by order of General Dodge; and General J. M. Corse, Chief of Staff to General Sherman, was assigned to the command.

The troops remained in the same position until the evening of the 26th of July, when General Sherman determined to move the Army of the Tennessee from the left to the right flank. To this end a very strong line of works had been built where the new left flank was to rest, in order to counteract an attack, should the enemy discover our withdrawal. All things being ready, as soon as it was dark, the 16th Corps silently left its works, first, followed by the 17th and 15th Corps, in order, but leaving the skirmishers to withdraw nearer daylight. The night was exceedingly dark, and the roads obscure and manifold, being close in rear of the army. We blundered along nearly all night, and at daylight went into bivouac for a few hours. We were still several miles from our destination, and began to move by ten o'clock. Some time in the afternoon, the 16th Corps began to go into position on the extreme right of the army on Utoy Creek. A brisk skirmish ensued, as our skirmishers drove back those of the enemy, and it was after dark before our troops got into position. The 17th Corps, which was to go on the right of the 16th, lay in rear that night in bivouac. On the 28th, it took position early, followed by the 15th Corps, which was to form the extreme right.

While the latter Corps was forming its line, Hood made another of his characteristic assaults. He had discovered our movement from left to right, and had undertaken to outmarch us, so as to get possession of the ground before we did. In this, as in his attack of the 22d, he was nearly successful. He had almost marched around the flank of our army, hence his attack fell mostly on the 15th Corps. It was like all the battles fought by Hood, bold and reckless. Mass after mass was hurled against the gallant 15th Corps, only to be horribly mangled and sent bleeding back. Still the attack was persistent, and General Howard, who the previous day had assumed command of the Army of the Tennessee, and who, with General Logan, was watching the contest, ordered up re-enforcements. From the 16th Corps four regiments were sent, two from Colonel Phillips' Brigade, 12th Illinois and 81st Ohio. These regiments arrived in time to not only revive the courage of the tried 15th Corps, but also to take an active part in repelling the enemy. This battle was known as the battle of Ebenezer Church. It was the last of Hood's attempts to "flank" General Sherman before Atlanta. Prisoners very generally said with more of truth than playfulness, that Hood could not fight much longer in that way, "for," said they, "he has not much more than one more killin' left!"

Now began what was in earnest, the siege of Atlanta. Our lines did not invest the place, but, as far as they reached, they were placed as close to the rebel works as possible. Whenever it was possible, some point in advance was seized by force or strategy, and thus we kept creeping closer and closer toward the stronghold. But it was a trying operation. Perhaps no month in the history of the 81st was filled with so much mental and bodily discomfort, as was this. It was hot; rations were barely sufficient, and sometimes scanty. Vegetables were not attainable. The troops actually had no rest. There were, in fact, no reserves where the enemy's balls did not come. It was a continued slow-fought battle, day and night for these four weeks. There was, to many of the regiments, less danger on the picket line than behind their works. The 81st was in such a position that its works afforded it no protection. Its members dug holes in the ground, and lived a sort of prison life there. The fly under which headquarters of the regiment was established was riddled with bullets, and if the place had not been strongly intrenched and sunk a little in the ground, it would have been untenable. Through the tree-tops, and against their trunks and limbs, the balls were continually flying. Every day some one or more were wounded or killed while walking about in camp, and more than one was killed while asleep at night. Other regiments were in like, or worse condition. Under these circumstances, men were becoming sick rapidly. Even the killed and wounded thinned the ranks sadly, but the continual watching and apprehension wore out the men worse than active duty could do. There was a growing necessity for some change of tactics. Every body saw that in this way Hood could soon be able to take Sherman instead of Sherman taking Atlanta.

About the first of August Governor Brough received official notice of the resignation of Colonel Morton and Major Evans. The former had remained as commandant at Pulaski until sometime in July, when, on account of bad health, he resigned. Major Evans remained with the regiment until after the investment of Kennesaw Mountain, when, being attacked violently with hemorrhage of the lungs, he was compelled to resign. Governor Brough filled the vacancies by appointing Lieutenant-Colonel R. N. Adams, Colonel, Captain J. W. Titus, Lieutenant-Colonel, and Captain W. H. Chamberlin, Major. Colonel Titus tendered his resignation in a few days, and it was accepted. Colonel Adams became ranking officer in the Brigade, and assumed command.

On the 20th of August, the 16th Corps lost the services of General Dodge, who had been so long connected with a part of that organization. The General was making, as was his invariable custom, a personal examination of that portion of his lines in front of General Corse's Division, accompanied by a single staff officer, and one or two orderlies. Not content with the view from the front line, he followed a little trench, cut for the purpose, to the outer intrenched picket line. Here, while looking through one of the loop-holes, a rebel sent a ball at him, and inflicted an ugly wound upon his forehead and the top of his head. Half an inch lower would have killed him. He was borne back to his quarters and sent North. Brigadier-General T. E. G. Ransom succeeded him in command.

About this time Captain W. H. Hill, of the 81st Ohio, while walking about in the camp of his regiment, received a very painful wound in his left hand, which rendered him unfit for duty, and he was sent North to hospital. Captain W. C. Henry succeeded to the command of the regiment.

During the advance of General Corse's lines one day, in this situation, Corporal Daniel Harpster, Company E, 81st Ohio, being on the skirmish line, ran out seventy-five yards in advance of his comrades, surprised a picket-post, where were intrenched four brawny, big rebels, and boldly demanded their surrender. The astonished Johnnies complied without a word! As he was about to march them to the rear, one of them asked him if they should bring their guns along. The anomaly of one man guarding four armed men seemed too great, and he directed them to leave their guns. They obeyed, and our little Corporal brought in those four giants of chivalry, all alone. If every officer and soldier in the army had always done his part as well as Corporal Harpster did on this occasion, the public would have had little cause to complain of our military operations.

CHAPTER XIV.

"ATLANTA OURS, AND FAIRLY WON."

On the 25th of August, Sherman's plans for his grand and decisive flank movement around Atlanta, were matured. That night Thomas' army, and a portion of the Army of the Tennessee, were withdrawn, and moved a short distance toward the right. All day of the 26th General Howard's command lay in nearly a circle, defending the then extreme left. The rebels were astonished and pleased, but they did not attack; they supposed General Sherman was in full retreat. On the night of the 26th, all of General Howard's Army of the Tennessee got fairly under way, and withdrew in perfect safety. It was a wearisome, hard march, as such night marches always were, but it was a relief to the men who had lain a whole month behind those hated works, and, weak as many of them were, they endured it cheerfully. Two men of the 81st Ohio, Sergeant James McCann, of Company C, and Private Frazer, of Company G, were lost in this movement, by lying down beside the road while the regiment made a temporary halt, and falling to sleep, did not wake until daylight, when they were aroused to be made prisoners. A heavy rain storm came up about one or two o'clock that night, but it caused no hindrance. The different Corps of the Army of the Tennessee moved by parallel roads, and by eight o'clock on the 27th, were encamped not far from the Sandtown ferry of the Chattahoochee. Resting here all day, the march was resumed on the 28th toward the railroad running from East Point to Montgomery, which was reached that night. The next day General Ransom, with a portion of his corps, spent the day in destroying the railroad from the vicinity of Fairburn, southward. His command destroyed about twelve miles effectually. Colonel Adams' Brigade distinguished itself by its rather extraordinary destructive abilities in this new field of action. But the pioneer corps of the 2d Division, composed mostly of contrabands, did the most effective service, and with the most good will. Hitherto these men had been employed in building bridges, repairing roads, and such work, which seemed to their woolly heads, to be rather aiding than injuring the South; but now, when an opportunity came of absolutely tearing up a great highway of rebeldom, their joy knew no bounds, and manifested itself in Herculean efforts at overturning long sections of the road at once, accompanied with songs and shouts of gladness. It is supposed that such an amount of labor was never before extracted from them in any other undertaking.

On the 30th of August the troops again moved, the arrangement of the whole army being such that, as usual, the Army of the Tennessee was on the outer flank, and did the most marching. This day the progress was much hindered by the enemy's cavalry, which, with one or two pieces of artillery, kept disputing our advance at every defensible point. At one time, one Brigade of infantry from General Corse's Division, was sent forward to aid General Kilpatrick's cavalry, and, in making a charge, the 2d and 7th Iowa regiments lost considerably. The orders were for the 16th Corps to reach, that night, a position on Flint river, near Jonesboro. Owing to these hindrances, and the fact that this Corps had to construct its own road for the last eight miles, the last of the command did not reach camp until almost daylight.

A portion of the 15th Corps which had arrived earlier the evening before, had crossed Flint river, and had encountered some of the enemy's pickets. Early in the morning of the 31st, General Corse's Division of the 16th Corps was moved across and placed in line on the right of the 15th Corps—Colonel Adams' Brigade joining the 15th Corps, and General Rice's Brigade on the right, which extended the line nearly to the river. In this position works were thrown up. In the meantime, General Sherman had arranged a programme for the day's exercises, comprising various movements. In the Army of the Tennessee, a demonstration was to be made as of an advance, about the middle of the afternoon. Other portions of the army were to tear up track, etc. But the rebels had their plans laid also, and that without consultation with General Sherman. The result was that just about the time General Howard was to make his demonstrations, the enemy came pouring upon the 15th and 16th Corps in an impetuous charge. Fierce and sharp was the attack, but Sherman's heroes had chosen their ground, and were determined to maintain it. The chief point of apprehension was that they would outflank us, as they evidently thought they could, on the right. To prevent this, General Ransom hurried over a Brigade from the 4th Division, and had it in readiness for such an emergency. But the rebel line was too short to reach beyond our flank, and too weak to pierce our living wall, so the battle ended with another victory for the Right. Our loss was almost nothing, while the rebel loss in killed was counted by hundreds. In front of Colonel Adams' Brigade they advanced through an open field, where our artillery and musketry poured volleys into their ranks, which cut them down by scores. When their line retreated, numbers refused to go back, and lay concealed until such time as they could rise with safety and surrender. From these prisoners we learned that it was General Pat. Cleburne's Division that had been thrown on the rebel left, and which had been so disastrously repulsed by General Corse's command.

After the fighting of this day was ended a stray ball from a rebel skirmisher flew over into the camp of the 2d Brigade, and falling under the fly at Headquarters, wounded Colonel Adams slightly. It was not serious enough to take him from duty.

The next day grand preparations were made for a literal squeezing together of the rebel army. It was known that but about two-thirds of it was at Jonesboro, and General Sherman felt able to envelop that army entirely with his own. He set the left to the task of driving in the enemy's right, and ordered the 17th Corps to our extreme right to drive in that flank. The plan was excellent, and General Jeff. Davis, of the 14th Corps, won his fame by carrying out his part of it successfully; but others were not so quick in their movements, and night came before the troops were all in position to make the grand attack. Morning of September 2d disclosed to us that the enemy had evacuated Jonesboro, and brought rumors that Slocum, who had all this time been left at the Chattahoochee river with the 20th Corps, had entered Atlanta !

The campaign was ended! For four months this army had been in march, bivouac or battle, without intermission. Now there would be a rest.

Nevertheless the order of that morning was forward! and southward the whole army started in pursuit. The enemy was overtaken at Lovejoy's Station, where the rebel Corps which had evacuated Atlanta, joined the remainder of the Army. General Sherman made a demonstration against them, but it was simply for effect. He did not wish to risk a general engagement. The 81st Ohio was sent out on the skirmish line here, and pressed so vigorously on the rebels that it lost several in killed and wounded.

If it had been properly supported its charge would have driven the enemy from their works in its front.

The retrograde march to Atlanta was conducted with great care. Strong works were built about a mile in rear of the advance line, and manned with the reserves, while those in front withdrew under cover of darkness. A tremendous rain fell the night the movement began, making it almost impossible to move artillery or wagons, but nevertheless the 16th Corps was able to withdraw, shortly after daylight of September 6th, from the reserve works, and to reach Jonesboro undisturbed. Here the troops resumed their old positions. The following morning General Howard's command moved again, reaching Rough and Ready that night, and the next day, September 8th, it reached East Point, where it was to be stationed.

The day after the battle of Jonesboro, Private M. R. Blizzard, of Company I, was wounded by a rebel ball while walking in front of our works. The wound proved fatal—the poor fellow died the third day. Young Blizzard had endeared himself to all his acquaintances by his quiet, manly bearing, and his excellent, soldierly qualities, and his death, just at the close of the hard campaign, seemed a mysterious dispensation.

During the progress of the campaign it had been unanimously supposed by officers and men, that after it was ended there would be a halt for the winter. Such had been the previous practice. Grant took Vicksburg on the 4th of July, and his army was furloughed and scattered from that time until the following spring. And there had not yet been a campaign as severe as this one. Therefore it was expected that as a matter of course the attainment of the objective point would be the beginning of a winter of comparative quiet. But General Sherman had other intentions, and in this case, as in many others, he did not think it necessary to keep them entirely secret. In his orders announcing the fall of Atlanta, and the assignment of the three armies to their positions at Decatur, Atlanta and East Point, he added that "the troops would now have *a full month's rest*, preparatory to a *fine winter's campaign!*" Unexpected as this announcement was, and uninviting as was the prospect it gave to many, the phrases "full month's rest," and "fine winter's campaign" became by-words that were provocative of many a good natured smile.

The 81st Ohio, trusting all things, ordered up the tents that had been left at Chattanooga, and having cleaned off a camping ground with great labor, pitched their tents and made themselves comfortable.

Just as the army left Atlanta on this final movement, the few men of the five old companies who had served three years, and who had not re-enlisted, started North to be mustered out. They numbered about one hundred and fifty, and their withdrawal did not necessarily change the organization of the regiment. There were still enough men to make a show of ten companies, and it was not till late in December that official notice of their muster out came; and even then only two companies (B and C) were mustered out entire, that is, lost their existence. The remaining members of those companies, veterans and recruits, were assigned to the other companies of the regiment.

CHAPTER XV.

THE MARCH FROM ATLANTA TO THE SEA.

September had not passed until evidences of the beginning of the "fine winter's campaign" began to appear. The 81st Ohio, with the remainder of General Corse's Division, was ordered to Rome, Georgia. One Brigade of that Division had been in garrison there ever since its capture in May. Here again the 81st pitched tents and hoped to abide. But this hope, like most of its predecessors, was rudely dispelled, and I believe that here ended the pitching of tents and establishment of permanent camps on the part of the 81st Ohio. It was to be taught new lessons in warfare; taught to have no abiding place; to despise the idle soldiers who dwelt in garrisons; to march as never they had marched, and to become invincible, not only in their own eyes, but in the eyes of the world. And what was of most consequence to the cause, they were to be taught to become irresistible against the enemy. So, at Rome, the dear old custom of dwelling in established camps was given up by the 81st Ohio forever.

About this time the command known as the Left Wing 16th Army Corps, comprising the 2d and 4th Divisions of the Corps, was put out of existence. General Dodge, who for so long a time had been its able commander, had not yet returned, being kept away by the effects of his severe wound. General Ransom, his successor, the brave, genial, gallant Illinoisan, had just died, literally at his post, and there was no one to plead for the old command. The unyielding, relentless axe of military necessity fell, and the Left Wing, 16th Army Corps, ceased to be. Its component parts were divided between the 17th and 15th Corps.

The 4th Division, General Fuller, went to the 17th Corps. The 2d Division, General Corse, was assigned to the 15th Corps, and its number was changed from 2d to 4th.

In October, Governor Brough made two appointments of field officers for the 81st. Captain W. H. Hill to be Lieutenant-Colonel, *vice* Titus resigned, and Captain W. Clay Henry to be Major, *vice* Chamberlin, resigned. As Colonel Hill was still absent North, in consequence of the wound he received before Atlanta, the command of the regiment remained with Major Henry, who had commanded it since some time in August.

Hood had now fairly begun his great work of forcing General Sherman back to Chattanooga. He sent French's Division to capture Allatoona, but that officer after fighting one of the bloodiest battles of the war, retired, discomfited by a single Brigade, under the gallant Corse. For a time there was much apprehension felt for the result of Hood's bold movement. Atlanta was left with a garrison of but a single Division, and the rest of Sherman's army was put in motion northward after Hood. General Corse's brilliant action at Allatoona proved that it was to be no easy task to subdue the men who had been the conquerors in the four months' battle just ended, and Hood's purposes were thwarted. He, however, made an attack at Resaca, and actually "repeated history" in an inverted manner, by displaying precisely the tactics shown by Sherman in May previous. After attacking Resaca he fell back to Snake Creek Gap, and occupied the works which we had built. But his plans required constant movement, as he had no railroad to supply his army, and hence, finding that he could effect nothing by attacks along the line of the railroad, he deflected westwardly into Alabama, where, after a brief pursuit, Sherman let him go to seek his own destruction, while he set about maturing preparations for his "grand march to the sea." In all these movements the 81st Ohio had remained at Rome, performing garrison duty.

On the 11th day of November, 1864, at 6 A. M., the 81st Ohio left Rome to begin the longest march ever yet attempted by our army. Passing a few miles beyond Kingston, the regiment encamped. The next day the march was continued a few miles beyond Allatoona. On the 13th it reached Marietta. There were by this time abundant evidences that there was to be no backward movement, and no communication with the rear. Rome, Kingston, Acworth and Marietta were more or less destroyed by fire; the railroad was torn up and surplus stores of our own were burned. On the 14th the regiment crossed the Chattahoochee and bivouacked at Turner's Ferry, and on the following day passed through Atlanta, encamping for the night four miles south of the city. Many members of the regiment took occasion to view again their battle ground, the graves of comrades, the works of both parties, the *dead line*, where the pickets waged their incessant warfare, and the "pits" in which they had lain for security in the time of the "siege." On this day the final destruction of Atlanta occurred. The bursting of shell in the depot buildings, the burning of the solid blocks in the business part of the town, the gratis distribution of clothing, which otherwise would have been burned, were all witnessed by the regiment; and at night, four miles away, the light of the still burning city was sufficient to enable them to read letters. The railroad, of course, was all destroyed; the Division train had been loaded with fifteen days' rations of hard bread, and *eighty of salt*. Every soldier who knew this fact, knew its significance—that it meant a long march without a base of supplies—a march through the enemy's country.

On the 16th of November, the 81st marched twenty-six miles, encamping eight miles south-west of Jonesboro.

Passing through McDonough and Jackson, the regiment reached the Ocmulgee river at a point called Ocmulgee Mills, and crossed in rear of the 15th Corps, on the 19th. Here a cotton factory and grist mill belonging to a bitter rebel, originally from the North, were burned. The owner stoutly disowned any displeasure, assuring our men that with all their vandalism, they could not hurt his pocket.

On the 21st, the 81st passed through Monticello and encamped a short distance from Hillsborough. The roads were in such awful condition from the continuous rain, that progress was slow. In the four days ending with the 21st, the regiment had marched but about thirty-two miles. There had been, however, an abundance of forage and provisions, and the men were in excellent spirits.

Following this period of rain and mud, came one of cold. On the morning of the 22d of November, ice was found a quarter of an inch in thickness. There was hard pulling for the teams, and a pontoon train, which marched that day before the 81st, stuck in the mud near Clinton, about sunset, and froze there, compelling the men to encamp in the road without wood or water. The next day the 81st aided the pontoon train out of its frozen condition and the roads improving, better time was made. On the 24th the regiment reached the Macon and Savannah Railroad at Gordon, which place was totally destroyed. This place is east of Macon, and south-west of Milledgeville, about equi-distant from both. Crossing the railroad, and moving south two miles on the Jeffersonville road, the troops encamped for the rest of the day, only having marched about six miles. It was the National Thanksgiving Day, and many a thought was turned Northward to the good dinners at home, while the boys, so far away, were taking their dinners in the bivouac. But there was far from a famine there: turkey, chicken, honey, sweet potatoes, corn cakes and other Southern delicacies graced the festal boards of "the conquerors" that day.

On the 25th, the march was resumed on the Irwinton road, the 81st passing through that town and burning the Court House and other public buildings, and also a lot of cotton. The next day the Oconee river was reached and crossed at Morning Ferry, on a pontoon bridge. Here our boys came in sight of growing palms, of which heretofore they had had knowledge only by the fans made from their leaves. Spanish Moss, another familiar article, was here seen growing. Here too, they were introduced to the Southern swamps; the land along the Oconee was found to be marshy. Emerging from the swampy land before night, a country of sand and pine forests was next reached Here the boys found abundance of pea nuts, just ready to be eaten.

On the 28th and 29th, Col. Adams' Brigade of General Corse's Division, enjoyed the luxury of getting lost. Being in advance of the Corps, Colonel Adams followed General Corse, who was following General Howard. The latter officer led them all astray. At night of the 28th they were fifteen miles away from the rest of the army, having passed all day through the most God-forsaken country they had yet seen. The whole route was through an immense pine forest with a swamp every mile of the way. The next day the troops moved through the same kind of country; the swamps are said to be the source of the Ohoopee river. This day they succeeded in getting on the right road, and in getting near other troops. These two days' march were made mostly in Johnson and Emanuel counties. The same unbroken pine forest continued through the next day's march, on which, the town of Somerville was passed. At night the regiment encamped not far from Herndon. December 1st they moved a few miles down the Ogeechee river and encamped near Millen. On the 2d and 3d a part of the Division operated on the railroad near Scarboro, and the 81st acted as a support. Here the first defensive works of this campaign were constructed. On the 4th the regiment moved south fifteen miles over good roads, and through finer country than it had passed since leaving Gordon, and encamped opposite Cameron. The 17th Corps was moving down on the left bank of the river, and became engaged with the enemy. The sound of their cannonading was distinctly heard by the 15th Corps. On the 6th the regiment encamped about thirty-five miles from Savannah. The country was of the best in the south, and the scenery such as the northern soldiers had never seen. "Live Oaks" in their evergreen beauty were abundant, and in addition to their foliage, the boughs of all the trees were gracefully festooned by the "Spanish Moss." In the midst of this wealth of natural loveliness, the red blossom of War was to re-appear to our heroes who had hitherto had a bloodless march.

On the 7th the regiment moved to a point opposite Eden, on the Savannah Railroad. The 1st Brigade of Gen. Corse's Division crossed the river and found a force of the enemy in their front. The gallant 2d Iowa charged and took a line of their works, capturing twenty-eight of their men. Its loss was two killed and five wounded. On the 8th the whole Division moved without supply train, but with two days' rations in their haversacks. They crossed the river, struck the railroad at Eden, and then moved south until they reached the Ogeechee Canal, near the Big Ogeechee river.

On the next day the Second Brigade was ordered to advance on the enemy, who occupied a well fortified position between the two Ogeechee rivers. The 66th Illinois was deployed as skirmishers, and the Brigade moved, coming upon the rebel works which were defended by a section of artillery. A charge was made resulting in the capture of one piece of artillery and a number of prisoners, and in driving the remainder until night. In this action, our loss was slight, the 81st Ohio losing none, the 66th and 12th Illinois each lost four men wounded. The enemy numbered about fifteen hundred, and had every advantage of position and works, but they were driven from them by the first efforts of our skirmish line. The same day the Brigade captured a train on the Savannah and Gulf Railroad with the President of the road and other passengers. The train was heard coming out from Savannah when it was a considerable distance away. Three mounted men were immediately dispatched to displace a rail in advance of the engine. They succeeded in doing their work; the train came on in front of the Brigade, whereupon a loose fire was opened upon it, which only served to increase the speed. Soon the engineer saw the break in the track and thinking to escape by running back into Savannah, he reversed and started back. The Brigade was too far away to prevent him by its fire, and he would have succeeded, but for the thoughtfulness of a soldier who happened to find a citizen's mule team near a road crossing. He drove the wagon on the track and shot the mules, forming a complete blockade. By the time the train reached this, re-inforcements came up and the train was a prize. Colonel Adams made prisoners of the male passengers, gallantly released the ladies unconditionally, and burned the cars.

Picket and slight reconnoisances occupied the time from the 9th until the 13th of December, on which day the 81st was ordered to take up a position and fortify. Moving out to the place designated, it was found to be but about seven hundred yards from one of the enemy's large forts. The enemy discovered the movement and threw shells. One of them struck Private Fletcher B. Haynes. Company C, on the shoulder and back, inflicting a wound of which he died on the 18th. This was the only loss sustained by the regiment in the whole campaign. On this day General Hazen opened communication with the fleet in Ossabaw Sound by the capture of Fort McAllister. Repeated efforts were made by Colonel Adams to find a crossing of the Little Ogeechee, which indeed, was a desirable object, as the enemy held the opposite side. On the night of the 13th, Companies E. and F. were detailed as a sort of forlorn hope to make the crossing at the Railroad Bridge. They found the bridge burning, and attempted to stop the flames, but after a number of them had gone on the bridge, a party of rebels on the opposite bank fired a volley into them which did no harm. The men of these companies then fell back behind the abutment, and thus, not more than thirty yards from the rebels, kept up a fire until they were able to get away unperceived.

From about the 12th of December, the troops began to feel the want of sufficient supplies. Lying as they did in close proximity, and in a country nearly covered with water, it was found to be impossible to keep the commissariat as full as when marching through a plenteous country. Corn meal was the sole article of food for several days, and after that, unhulled rice was the simple diet of the army for nearly a week. Although General Hazen had opened communication on the 13th, and the soldiers had evidence of it in the very welcome mail that began to arrive on the 16th, yet owing to the difficulties of transportation in that tide and swamp covered country, it was impossible to bring up supplies. No wonder then that the troops looked anxiously forward to the capture of Savannah.

At 9 P. M. of the 19th, Lieutenant Pittman with ten men, succeeded in effecting a crossing of the Little Ogeechee.

The boat he used—the only one that could be found—was brought to him that night by Captain McCain, assisted by Sergeant Charles Brennan, Corporal William L. Ward and Private Jamison Mayberry, of Company E, and Private William E. Walker, of Company H, who had volunteered to take the terrible risk of floating in it a mile and a half down the Ogeechee river, between the Rebel and Union picket lines, passing so near a rebel fort as to be able to hear distinctly their conversation. But, by good fortune, the daring little party passed in safety, and brought the much needed boat to Lieutenant Pittman. He explored the ground—Sergeant Mason and two men actually getting in rear of the enemy—and reported that a crossing by a force could easily be made. On receiving Lieutenant Pittman's report, Colonel Adams desired to cross with his Brigade, but General Osterhaus would not permit it.

On the morning of the 21st of December, the 81st Ohio, with the rest of the Brigade, had the extreme satisfaction of marching into the city of Savannah. General Hardee had, during the previous night, evacuated the place, leaving large amounts of munitions of war to fall into our hands. Thus was ended successfully, Sherman's grand march "from Atlanta to the Sea"—a march which will ever be memorable in history as the boldest and most extraordinary on record. Well may the veterans who composed that army, lift their heads in just pride in recollection of the part they took in this famous march.

The 81st Ohio in this campaign, marched over three hundred miles, starting from Rome. It was entirely without communication with the North from the 14th of November until the 16th of December. There were, in this time, about twenty-five marching days, averaging nearly fifteen miles a day, yet in all this time, there was no loss, except one, mortally wounded before Savannah, on the 13th of December.

On the 23d of December, the regiment went into camp on the Thunderbolt Road, near the city, and the next day, the 15th Army Corps was reviewed in the city, by General Sherman. It was a triumphal march—a stinging eye-sore to the resident rebels who from their closed windows stole views of their hated conquerors.

Now came a brief season of rest. From the fatigue of the march, and the starving of the last few days before communication was fully established, Savannah was a welcome resting place. In addition to the full fare granted by a liberal "Uncle Sam," the boys had such feasts of oysters and fresh fish as many of them had never dreamed of. Supplies of clothing were issued, long letters were written home, telling each to an interested group away North, how the writer bore his part in the "great march," and every arriving vessel brought rich, full mail sacks that were as good as gold to these far off soldiers. So the time wore on: fatigue duty now and then in building new defenses to the city; absolute rest for many days, another review on the 7th of January, and finally, on the 17th, the portentous order to be ready to move at a moment's notice.

On the 8th of January, General Logan resumed command of the 15th Corps. He had a leave of absence after the fall of Atlanta, and did not re-join the army before Sherman broke loose from his communications; so he had to sail to Savannah to meet his command. General Osterhaus commanded the Corps during the march.

CHAPTER XVI.

THROUGH THE CAROLINAS TO PEACE.

On the 19th of January, 1865, the 81st Ohio moved from Savannah, crossing the Savannah river on pontoons to Hutchinson's Island, but owing to the unprecedented rain, it was found impossible to proceed in that direction, and the regiment returned to its old quarters the same day. Rain fell for several days, and the movement seemed indefinitely delayed. However, on the 28th of January, the 81st Ohio —the last regiment of Sherman's army in the city—moved out and marched to near Eden. In the next two days the march was continued northward, and the regiment, at the end of that time, reached Sister's Ferry, on the Savannah river.

On the evening of February 4th, the regiment crossed the Savannah river into South Carolina at Sister's Ferry. The event of entering upon the sacred soil of South Carolina was signalized by the army in a way that showed how they appreciated the active part that State had taken in the inauguration of secession and civil war. Every man seemed to foreknow that the day of retribution had come, and that this army was to be the avenging instrument. As the regiments set foot on the soil of the Palmetto State, they began cheering long and loud, and kept it up continuously for several hours. If the spirit of Treason could have heard that shout, it would certainly have known that it was its death-knell.

The beginning of this march presented difficulties which grew and continued almost throughout its entire length. The Savannah campaign had been made with scarcely any organized enemy to hinder the march; but here, in addition to the natural obstacles, the collected forces of the now bisected Confederacy were at hand to take possession of every river and other defensible position in the country. But this was the least of Sherman's troubles. The route was over a country which the rebel Generals have since declared they believed to be impracticable for an army to pass. Evidences of this came with the first day's march. Heavy details were made to build corduroy roads through the swamp, and at night the men encamped but a few miles from their starting place, wearied with the heavy labor. The enemy's cavalry was watchful, too, and picked off whatever stragglers they could find. They took no prisoners. On the 6th, the mounted foragers of Colonel Adams' Brigade came upon two murdered soldiers belonging to the 20th Army Corps.

Having passed through Robertsville, the regiment reached Hickory Hill P. O., on the 7th, and crossed there a swamp of one mile in width, dignified by the name of Coosawatchie river. On the 9th the regiment reached the Salkehatchie river, at River's Bridge, where Generals Mower and Smith, with their Divisions of the 17th Corps, made a charge through water waist deep, and drove the enemy from their position. On the 10th of February better roads were reached, and on the smooth table-land a march of twenty-two miles was made, the regiment passing Buford's Bridge. The whole army was now concentrated along the Charleston and Augusta Railroad, which was effectually destroyed.

Taking the Orangeburg road, on the 11th, the regiment again made a good march, still on the table-lands, and crossed the South Edisto river at Benaker's Bridge. On the 12th, they reached the North Edisto river, where the enemy was posted to dispute the crossing; but the next morning a skirmish line cleared the way, and the troops crossed about three miles from Orangeburg. Taking the main

Columbia road, the regiment marched eighteen miles through a "tar and turpentine" region, encamping at night at Little Beaver Creek. On the 15th, the regiment reached Congaree Creek, where the enemy contested the crossing of the advance of the Corps. This was but five miles from Columbia.

On the 16th, the Congaree being crossed, the whole Corps moved across the plain in full view of the city, and formed line of battle, the right resting on the Congaree River, and the left on the Saluda. Considerable skirmishing and shelling ensued, but the main line did not become engaged. On the next day the city was formally surrendered by the Mayor.

After passing through Columbia, there were several days of destruction of railroad and of slow and circuitous marching. On the 24th, Colonel Adams was sent with his Brigade, with instructions to take Camden and destroy public property there. Not long after leaving the main column, he encountered some of the enemy's cavalry, which he steadily drove for a distance of five miles. One company of cavalry was assigned to him, which he used to protect his flanks. By a little rashness of theirs, fourteen of these were captured by the enemy. Throwing forward a heavy skirmish line, supported by the 12th Illinois, Colonel Adams placed the 66th Illinois in reserve, and sent the 81st Ohio on another road for the purpose of preventing an attack in the rear. By this time the enemy had taken a position in his front, behind a barricade on "Hobkirk's Hill," of Revolutionary interest. Having all things ready, Colonel Adams ordered forward! and, after skirmishing a short time, a charge, which was gallantly and successfully made. Gaining the hill, he continued the charge, now turned into a pursuit, through the streets of the town, capturing twelve of the enemy and re-capturing the fourteen cavalry men who had been lost that day. Even the citizens were armed, and fired at the troops as they entered the town. He immediately began the work of destruction, burning a large depot of commissary stores, consisting of flour, meal, bacon, sugar, &c. He also committed to the tender mercies of the flames two thousand bales of cotton and other property. Colonel Adams' command found plenty of good cheer, and the inhabitants made lavish offers of good things to eat and drink, which the hungry soldiers accepted, asking no questions. Leaving Camden that night, the Brigade joined the main column the next day.

On the 25th, the regiment encamped at "Pine Tree Meeting House," on Little Lynch's Creek. The next day they marched to Tiller's Bridge, where a crossing was made. The stream was nearly a mile wide, and was rising so that the trains could not cross. The troops, however, waded over, enjoying many a hearty laugh as the mounted officers were thrown headlong from their horses into the water.

On this day, the mounted foragers of the 2d Brigade were in a sharp skirmish. About five hundred rebel cavalry attacked them as they were returning across Lynch's Creek with their wagons loaded with forage. Making a stubborn defense, they saved the wagons, although they had a hand to hand struggle. Corporal Elijah Davis, Company I, 81st Ohio, received five sabre cuts about the head. Our boys were opportunely re-enforced by the foragers of the 1st and 3d Brigades, and the rebels were driven off with the loss of sixteen killed and some prisoners.

The bridging of this stream required some time, and it was not until March 1st that the trains had crossed, and the movement was continued. The regiment moved but eight miles, and encamped on Black Creek. On the 2d, the regiment did not move, General Howard retaining it as a guard for his Head Quarters, but on the 3d, it marched twenty miles on the Cheraw road, encamping at Thompson's Creek. The next day it went into camp on the Pedee River, one mile from Cheraw. On the 6th, the regiment moved through Cheraw, halting a while in the streets. There had been, during the previous day or two, a large amount of ammunition and powder thrown into ditches, and other places where it could be destroyed. A large quantity, it seems, was thrown into one gully and was not yet dampened. Near it small quantities of loose powder were lying on the ground, which the soldiers were burning for their amusement. By some means the large quantity was ignited, and there was a tremendous explosion.

Surgeon W. C. Jacobs thus writes of it:

"Chips, mud, sticks and stones fell in every direction; the smoke for a time hid every thing from view, and I found myself going up street at no very dignified pace. Upon examination I found I was not hurt, and then I began to look for the wounded. Lawrence Smith, of Company D, 81st Ohio, was crushed to death by a falling building. Corporal Wyman, of the same company, had a leg fractured. It is estimated that at least three tons of powder were consumed in the explosion. Not a window was left unbroken in the town."

On the 7th of March, the regiment moved on the Fayetteville road ten miles, and encamped at Goodwin's Mills. The next day the regiment passed through a little town called Springfield, and soon after crossed the line between North and South Carolina. As soon as the old North State was entered, guards were placed at each house as the column passed, with strict instructions to allow no one whatever to enter, but soldiers were not prohibited from taking provisions from out-houses. This was in deference to the supposed loyalty of these people.

On the 9th, there was a harassing and wearisome march through rain and mud. Laurel Hill was passed, and so muddy were the roads, that when night overtook the trains, they found it impossible to proceed, and so, corralled in the road or alongside, wherever they could find the ground solid enough to keep them from sinking out of sight. The next day, Lumber River was crossed, and the Brigade went into camp early, sending the 12th Illinois forward to repair road. Wretched as were the roads and the weather, yet, as the troops knew they were marching toward the North and toward communications with the "cracker line," as well as with their friends at home, they performed the heaviest labor with great cheerfulness. Realizing the necessity of the work, they felt and manifested a pride in being equal to the great occasion.

On the 11th, the regiment moved over about sixteen miles, eleven of which were corduroy. The whole surface of the country seemed to be covered with water. This road is said to be the same that General Greene made in 1776. Encamped on Little Fish Creek, thirteen miles from Fayetteville. On the 12th, a march of fourteen miles brought the regiment to its camping place near Fayetteville. Here supplies were received, and New York papers of the 6th, containing much news of great interest from the outer world.

On the 15th, the regiment moved in the direction of Goldsboro', reaching South River, where the 7th Iowa and Battery H, First Missouri Light Artillery had a slight engagement with the enemy, who disputed the crossing with a small force and one piece of artillery. On the next day the 81st Ohio had the advance of the whole Corps. Crossing South River, they had advanced but a few miles over miserable roads, until they encountered the enemy, and a spirited skirmish ensued. As soon, however, as Battery "H" opened, the enemy left. Corporal Samuel T. Wiley, 81st Ohio, was wounded in the knee, which was the only damage sustained by the regiment. Encamped that night at Ray's Church. On the 17th, a short march was made to Beaman's Cross Roads. The next day the regiment moved to a point within 28 miles of Goldsboro, passing through a very abundant country—a state of affairs highly acceptable to the men, as the scanty supply of rations received at Fayetteville was already exhausted.

The 19th of March was a battle day. Johnston had concentrated his forces with the bold attempt of thwarting Gen. Sherman and impeding his march. General Slocum encountered him first, and the heavy and rapid cannonading told that it was no mere skirmish. There was a rapid concentration of General Sherman's forces. Passing Falling Creek Church, the regiment marched until 10 P. M., and then threw up a line of works. The whole Corps was encamped that night in line of battle. The enemy had, during the day, made several bold but unsuccessful charges on Slocum. On the 20th, the whole line moved, so that before night, General Sherman's army was in a semi-circular line completely enveloping Johnston, except his rear, which was cut off by the Neuse River. The left of the army, consisting of the 14th Army Corps, joined on the Neuse, above Bentonville, while the 17th Army Corps touched the river below, and the 15th and 20th were in close connection between. Thus Johnston was put upon the defensive, and as Schofield and Terry were coming up, it was hoped he would soon be completely surrounded.

On the 21st, the lines of the 4th Division, 15th Corps, were advanced four hundred yards, to near Mill Creek, and new works were thrown up, under heavy fire from the enemy. Here, Robert McDill, Company I, was wounded in the knee, requiring amputation. Heavy skirmish firing continued until after dark. First Sergeant John M. Henness was slightly wounded in the arm, and Privates Finical and Burwell, of Company K., were badly wounded, while in the trenches, by an accidental shot from a gun in the hands of one of their comrades. The loss in the Brigade was two killed and ten wounded. During the night of the 21st, the enemy evacuated their works and crossed the Neuse.

On the 22d, General Sherman issued the following congratulatory order:

Head Quarters, Military Division of the Mississippi,
In the Field near Bentonville, N. C., March 22, 1865.

The Commanding General announces to this Army that yesterday it beat on its chosen ground the concentrated armies of our enemy, who has fled in disorder, leaving his dead, wounded and prisoners in our hands, and burning the bridge in his rear.

On the same day, Major General Schofield, from Newbern, entered and occupied Goldsboro, and Major General Terry, from Wilmington, secured Cox's Bridge crossing, and laid a pontoon bridge across Neuse River. So that our campaign has resulted in a glorious success, after a march of the most extraordinary character, of near five hundred miles over swamps and rivers deemed impassable to others, at the most inclement season of the year, and drawing our chief supplies from a poor and wasted country.

I thank the army, and assure it that our Government and people honor them for this new display of the physical and moral qualities which reflect honor upon the whole nation.

You shall now have rest, and all the supplies that can be brought from the rich granaries and storehouses of our magnificent country, before again embarking on new and untried dangers. W. T. SHERMAN,
Major General Commanding

On the 24th, the Army of the Tennessee reached Goldsboro, passing in review through the town. Perhaps there never was a review like this one. The men were just from their unparalleled march of five hundred miles, and were in all kinds of uniform and want of uniform. Many were without shoes, hats, coats, and some wore pants all too short. In the 81st Ohio, the shoeless and hatless men were all placed in one company, and in this manner passed in review before Sherman, Schofield, Terry, Howard and Logan, with more pride than their more fortunate comrades who wore shoes and hats. The army encamped near the city, and, of course, constructed defensive works.

In the brief rest which followed, rations soon made their appearance, and mail came again, gladdening the hearts of the soldiers. With the first mail came a number of commissions for officers and men of the 81st Ohio. Absentees and recruits here joined the regiment, coming around by way of New York.

The 81st Ohio, although but a fraction of a regiment for more than a year in the beginning of its existence, had the good fortune, in 1862 to receive more recruits than almost any other regiment in the service. Again, in 1864, enough recruits were obtained to keep up the waste so far, and now, in 1865, such a large number was obtained, that two entire new companies were formed, besides furnishing some men to the old companies. The two new companies were designated B and C, and filled the gap which had existed since the muster out of those companies in 1864. The raising of these last recruits was due mainly to the untiring energy of Lieutenant-Colonel W. H. Hill, who, being compelled to remain North during all the fall and winter, in consequence of his wound, and of the impossibility of reaching the army, devoted his attention to securing as many recruits as possible for the regiment. When these recruits joined the regiment it was again swelled to a size unlike any other regiments in the field, and was able to show fuller ranks at the end of the war than almost any other four years' regiment suffering as many losses.

On the 10th of April, the regiment marched toward Raleigh, going the first day as far as Pikeville. It was a day, or rather a night, long to be remembered. The roads were in a wretched condition, and Colonel Adams' Brigade was in charge of the train, with instructions to bring it into camp before stopping. The men were nearly all detailed to aid the sinking wagons, and to repair the roads. Night came, and still the train was a long distance behind. Colonel Adams reported the state of affairs, with a view to getting orders to encamp and rest, but he received positive orders to bring the train into Pikeville. He dispatched orderlies to hurry up the command, while he and a portion of his staff and escort went a short distance ahead, and built fires to light the way. While one of these orderlies was returning, he was killed by some rebel cavalry that were prowling along the way. Another was captured, but afterward made his escape. It was afterward ascertained that Wheeler's cavalry command, was but a short distance away, and was only prevented from falling on the train through ignorance of their opportunity. It was one o'clock before the train was pulled through, and the men laid down to rest.

On the 11th of April, the regiment reached Saucer-eye Creek, and on the next day, at Lowell's, heard of the surrender of Lee's army. That night it encamped near Cedar Town. On the 13th, it crossed Neuse River, and on the 14th passed through Raleigh and went into camp. The following day it marched to Morrisville, where it lay until the 21st, while General Sherman was negotiating with Johnston, and then marched back to Raleigh.

* * * * * * * *

The work was done! the long agony over! the War was ended! But no pen can tell the feeling of joy and triumph that flooded every heart in the army, as the war-worn soldiers looked forward to Peace and Home. In all this army there was not a man who did not justly feel that he had performed a hero's part in the closing acts of the war.

Marching victoriously from Atlanta to the Sea, and through the Carolinas to Peace, they had challenged the admiration of the world, and had achieved distinction in all future history. It was fitting that such grand achievements should culminate in so desirable a result as the utter overthrow of the Rebellion; and though the glad song of triumph and victory was hushed by the sad story of the foul murder of him who had been their leading star of hope and promise through all these years of conflict, it had but sanctified their work, and proved beyond all doubt, that the Treason they had just crushed was the sum of all crimes. By the assassination of President Lincoln the army was made to see how intimately he had been connected with them in the struggle, and how his blood was now mingled with that of the hosts who during the war had given their lives as the price of the unity of our Government.

> "Through our night of bloody struggle,
>   Ever dauntless, firm and true,
> Bravely, gently forth he led us,
>   Till the morn burst on our view—
> Till he saw the day of triumph,
>   Saw the field our heroes won;
> Then his honored life was ended,
>   Then his glorious work was done."

There is little more to write. The war being ended, there was no more thought of campaigning. The 29th of April had become a historic day with the 81st Ohio. In 1862, on that day was commenced the march from Pittsburg Landing, on the Corinth Campaign. In 1864, on that day, the regiment started from Pulaski, Tennessee, on the Atlanta campaign; and now, in 1865, on the 29th of April, the 81st started on its "homeward" march. No need to recall the incidents of this march. There was no war, and no foraging—no guards on the look out for an enemy, no burning of fences; it was simply a race to see what Corps should march to Washington first. The 81st Ohio reached its camp near Washington on the 20th of May. The next three days were spent in preparation for the grand review. On the 24th, this grandest of military pageants was seen in Washington. On that day Sherman's army was reviewed. It is said by good authority that never before did the gallant old 81st make so fine an appearance as on this, the last great field day. With steady step, and firm straight forward look, the men marched with such regular lines as to challenge again and again, the admiration of the crowds who thronged the streets, and who expressed their appreciation by repeated cheers.

Early in June the regiment started to Louisville, going by the Baltimore and Ohio Railroad to Parkersburgh, thence by the Ohio River. Encamping at Woodlawn near the city, the boys enjoyed themselves as best they could, until at last, came the welcome order to muster the regiment out of the service. This work was completed on the 13th of July, and the regiment immediately started to Camp Dennison to be paid and discharged. On the 21st of July this last act was completed, and the 81st Ohio was no more.

Thus we have followed the fortunes of this regiment from its first scouting over the prairies of Missouri; through its bloody baptism at Shiloh; its march into Mississippi; its participation in the battles of Iuka and Corinth; its garrison duty at the latter place; its march into Northern Alabama; its brief stay at Pocahontas; its march to Pulaski, and duty there; its deeds and privations in the historic Atlanta campaign; its march to Rome; its journey to the sea; and, finally, its march from Savannah to Raleigh, Washington, Louisville and Camp Dennison, whence each man went his way to his home, a citizen. It may be truly said that in all these scenes and actions, the 81st ever bore an honorable part. No stain rests upon the courage or devotedness of the men whose deeds are here recorded.

CHAPTER XVII.

THE RANK AND FILE OF THE EIGHTY-FIRST OHIO.

In the following pages are given the names of all the officers and enlisted men ever connected with the regiment, so far as it has been possible to obtain them. The records of Captain Kinsell's and Captain Hughes' companies could not be found, and hence some names of those who died or were discharged from these companies, before the consolidation in 1862, do not appear.

In the list of casualties no names of deserters are given. There were but twenty-three of them in the regiment during its entire term of nearly four years' service, exclusive of those in the two companies organized in 1865. It was not thought best to mar this Record of the gallant and faithful *many* by placing on it the names and crime of the cowardly and recreant *few*.

It will be observed that the record of companies D, E, F and K are not so full as that of the others. If any member of these companies feels aggrieved by the omission of any part of his military history, he must cast the blame where it belongs. Every effort was made to obtain the necessary facts from those companies, but without success; and finally I was compelled to resort to the muster-out rolls.

OFFICERS AND NON-COMMISSIONED OFFICERS OF THE FIELD AND STAFF.

Colonel THOMAS MORTON, appointed Aug. 19, '61; resigned July 30, 1864.

Colonel ROBERT N. ADAMS, promoted from Lieutenant-Colonel, Aug. 12, 1864; appointed Brevet Brigadier-General, to date from Mar. 13, '65; mustered out with the regiment July 13, '65.

Lieutenant-Colonel JOHN A. TURLEY, appointed Aug. 19, '61; resigned Dec. 1, '61.

Lieutenant Colonel R. N. ADAMS, promoted from Captain May 7, '62; promoted as above.

Lieutenant-Colonel JAMES W. TITUS, promoted from Captain Aug. 21, '64; resigned Sept. 8, '64.

Lieutenant-Colonel W. H. HILL, promoted from Captain Apr. 22, '65; mustered out with the regiment.

Major CHARLES N. LAMISON, appointed Aug. 19, '61; resigned Apr. 22, '62.

Major FRANK EVANS, promoted from Adjutant May 18, '62; resigned June 27, '64.

Major WILLIAM H. CHAMBERLIN, promoted from Captain Aug. 12, '64; resigned Sept. 15, '64.

Major WILLIAM C. HENRY, promoted from Captain Nov. 1, '64; mustered out with the regiment.

Surgeon WILLIAM H. LAMME, appointed Nov. 27, '61; resigned Mar. 31, '62.

Surgeon ROBERT G. MCLEAN, promoted from Assistant Surgeon Mar. 31, '62; resigned Nov. 6, '62.

Surgeon WILLIAM C. JACOBS, appointed Dec. 23, '62; mustered out with the regiment.

Assistant Surgeon ROBERT G. MCLEAN, appointed Nov. 20, '61; promoted as above.

Assistant Surgeon JOHN WHITTAKER, appointed Aug. 19, '62; resigned Nov. 11, '64.

Assistant Surgeon HIRAM SHAFFER, appointed Mar. 19, '63; mustered out on expiration of term of service, Aug. 24, '64.

Chaplain JAMES YOUNG, appointed Feb. 11, '63; resigned Dec. 26, '63.

Adjutant FRANK EVANS, appointed Aug. 19, '61; promoted as above.

Adjutant JOHN R. HUNT, appointed Sept. 9, '62; resigned Sept. 24, '64.

Adjutant CORNELIUS C. PLATTER, promoted from 2d Lieutenant and appointed Adjutant Nov. 1, '64; promoted to Captain and assigned to Company D Mar. 28, '65.

Adjutant WILLIAM B. RUSH, promoted from Sergeant-Major and appointed Adjutant Mar. 28, '65; mustered out with the regiment.

Quartermaster SAMUEL E. ADAMS, appointed Aug. 19, '61; mustered out on expiration of term of service, Aug. 18, 1864.

Quartermaster W. A. JOHNSON, promoted from 2d Lieutenant June 27, '64; promoted to Captain and assigned to Company F May 25, '65.

Quartermaster JOHN N. HAYS, promoted from Quartermaster Sergeant Mar. 26, '65; appointed Quartermaster Apr. 25, 65; mustered out with the regiment.

Non-commissioned Staff mustered out with the Regiment July 13, 1865.—Sergeant-Major CHARLES W. FOGLE; Quartermaster Sergeant JOHN T. COLLIER; Hospital Steward CHARLES SHOCK; Principal Musicians JOHN H. BUELTEL and WILLIAM N. MILLER; Commissary-Sergeant JOSEPH S. CAMPBELL.

Casualties in Non-commissioned Staff.

Died.—GEORGE K. HAGERMAN, Principal Musician, at Columbia, South Carolina, Feb. 17, '65.

Discharged to accept Promotion.—Sergeant-Majors—JOHN R. CHAMBERLIN, promoted to 2d Lieutenant Apr. 29, '63, discharged on account of physical disability Apr. 6, '64; WILLIAM PITTMAN, promoted to 2d Lieutenant June 20, 1864; WILLIAM M. MURPHY, promoted to 2d Lieutenant Aug. 15, '64; WILLIAM B. RUSH, promoted to 1st Lieutenant Mar. 26, '65; SUMNER F. MASON, promoted to 2d Lieutenant May 24, '65. Commissary-Sergeant C. B. VAN PELT, promoted to Quartermaster-Sergeant Mar. 26, 1865. Quartermaster-Serg'ts—CORNELIUS C. PLATTER, promoted to 2d Lieutenant June 27, '64; THOMAS J. HARBAUGH, promoted to 2d Lieutenant Aug. 19, '64; JOHN N. HAYS, promoted to 1st Lieutenant Mar. 26, '65; CORWIN B. VAN PELT, promoted to 2d Lieutenant May 24, '65.

Discharged upon Expiration of Term of Service.—Hospital Stewards—DAVID W. LAMME, Dec. 12, '64, and WILLIAM D. STEPHENS, May 25, '65. Principal Musicians—RICHARD LAYCOX, Oct. 7, '64, and ASBURY L. STEPHENS, May 26, '65.

Discharged for Disability.—Quartermaster-Sergeant WALKER W. MCCLAIN, Feb. 17, '62, and Commissary-Sergeant ANDREW R. BOGGS; place and date not known.

No Record Found.—Commissary-Sergeant P. B. AYERS.

Returned to Company.—Commissary-Sergeant DAVIS E. JAMES, May, 1864.

ORIGINAL MEMBERS OF COMPANY A, 81ST OHIO, ORGANIZED AT LIMA, ALLEN COUNTY, OHIO, SEPTEMBER, 1862, BY CAPTAIN W. H. HILL.

Captain WILLIAM H. HILL, First Lieutenant DAVID S. VAN PELT, Second Lieutenant TIMOTHY SHAFFER.

Sergeants.—First Sergeant Adam C. Post; Joseph H. Harbison, Charles W. Fogle, George W. Enboden, Theodore G. McDonald.

Corporals.—William P. DeHart, William A. J. Moorman, William M. Lochhead, Richard W. Vance, Fielding Tonguet, John Hill, William Adams, Samuel Martin.

Musicians.—William Miller, Hervey Wicks.

Teamster.—Hiram Armitage.

Privates.—Irwin Allspaw, Benjamin F. Allison, Hamiline Bice, William Bennett, Andrew Brenning, William Boyer, Jesse W. Baird, David B. Buckles, George W. Biner, John A. Bird, Isaac Counts, Emanuel Carolus, George W. Carey, William Culver, Samuel P. Cheatwood, George H. Cheatwood, Wesley Coon, James Cook, Abraham Decoursey, James Davis, Andrew Davis, Alexander Emmons, John Eisenbice, Ferdinand Eisenbice, Joseph J. Ferl, Joseph I. Fair, Isaac Gatton, James S. Garver, William R. Gordon, Henry Garee, Lorenzo D. Harter, Charles E. Hogue, Allen Jamison, David Lee, Peter Lies, Solomon B. Miller, Martin Miller, Tobias Miller, Solomon P. Miller, Isaac N. Miller, Henry C. Miller, Jacob M. Moorman, Thomas Moorman, Madison Moorman, Antel J. Moorman, James May, Samuel Mottier, John McMullin, William Place, James Point, Andrew J. Point, Loveman Place, William Perry, Henry Pool, Samuel Rider, Joseph H. Rider, John N. Rupert, Alanson S. Rhodes, Benjamin C. Seaman, Samuel Shock, Charles W. Smith, Walter S. Stevens, Robert Sutton, Ebenezer Sunderland, Samuel Sunderland, Andrew D. Sunderland, Robert Sunderland, Abraham Shanks, Benjamin F. Simkins, Samuel L. Sweeney, John Terwilliger, Elijah Tracy, Washington Tippie, Corwin B. Van Pelt, Rufus White, Isaac Walters, George W. Winans, William H. Winans, Thomas Whetstone, Aaron Zircle.

Recruits.—Frederick Conkel, Alexander C. Counts, Thos. Fair, Francis M. Harter, Bennett Harter, Barton S. Harter, John Miller, Eli Miller, Warrick W. Morton, George A. Park, Clark Ely, Peter Ely, George Hammond, John Meaker, Leroy Place, Edgar Stevens.

CASUALTIES,

Promotions.—Captain W. H. HILL to Lieutenant-Colonel, April 22, '65; First Lieutenant, D. S. VAN PELT, to Captain, May 17, '64; First Sergeant, Adam C. Post, to Second Lieutenant, June 19, '64; to First Lieutenant, April 23, '65; Sergeant, Joseph H. Harbison to First Sergeant, June 19, '64; to Second Lieutenant, May 24, '65; Private Corwin B. Van Pelt, to Commissary Sergeant, July 1, '64; to Quartermaster Sergeant, March 26. '65; to Second Lieutenant, May 24, '65.

Died of Disease.—Albert G. Gatton, Corinth, Miss., Jan. 13, '63; Thomas Whetstone, Corinth, Miss., Feb. 5, '63; Samuel Shock, Corinth, Miss., March 12, '63; William A. J. Moorman, Corinth, Miss., April 18, '63; Joseph I. Fair, Corinth, Miss., April 28, '63; William Culver, Pocahontas, Tenn., July 6, '63; Hamiline Bice, Corinth, Miss., July 18, '63; Thomas Moorman, Pocahontas, Tenn. Aug. 8, '63; Warrick W. Morton, Pulaski, Tenn., March 17, '64; Thomas Fair, Chattanooga, Tenn., May 27, '64; Henry Sunderland, Rome, Ga., July 4, '64; Francis M. Harter, Marietta, Ga., Sept. 3, '64; Hiram Armitage, Rome, Ga., Sept. 3, '64; Sergeant Wm. P. De Hart, Lima, O., Dec. 16, '64; William Adams, Chattanooga, Tenn., Nov. 16, '64; James S. Cook, Louisville, Ky., Dec. 16, '64; George W. Winans, Rome, Ga., Sept. 10, '64.

Discharged for Disability.—Elijah Tracy, Oct. 23, '62; Wm. H. Winans, Jan. 7, '63; Hervey Wicks, Jan. 14, '63; James Davis, Jan. 14, '63; James S. Garver, Jan. 21, '63; Henry Pool, March 27, '63; George W. Enboden—no date; Loveman Place, Jan. 24, '63; David B. Buckles, Jan. 19, '65; Isaac Gatton, March 16, '65; Samuel Mottier, May 19, '65; William Perry, May 30, '65; George A. Park, May 5, '65; Geo. W. Smith, May 5, '65.

Discharged to accept Promotion.—John Terwilliger, Sept. 14, '63.

Discharged upon Expiration of Term of Service.—R. K. Darling, Sept. 6, '64.

Transferred—To Non-commissioned Staff, Corwin B. Van Pelt, July 1, '64; Chas. W. Fogle, May 24, '65; W. N. Miller, May 26, '65; to Veteran Reserve Corps, Madison Moorman, Oct. 7, '64.

Resigned.—Second Lieut., Timothy Shaffer, Aug. 24,' 64.

ORIGINAL MEMBERS OF COMPANY B, 81ST OHIO, ORGANIZED AT LIMA, OHIO, AUGUST, 1861, BY CAPTAIN M. ARMSTRONG.

Captain MARTIN ARMSTRONG, First Lieutenant, JAMES W. TITUS, Second Lieutenant WILLIAM F. WILCOX.

Sergeants.—First Sergeant, James H. Corns; George W. Dixon, George W. Miller, Rufus K. Darling, John Johnson.

Corporals.—Gideon Ditto, Jerome Raymond,* Wallace Standish, Sumner F. Mason, John B. Jacobs, John Askins, Francis M. Hartshorn, William D. Cunningham.

Privates—John W. Armour, Madison W. Alexander,* G. H. Adgate, John W. Anderson, Abraham Bumgardner, Jasper Buckmaster, Thomas D. Crosley, Gabriel Coffman, William Copas, Eli Champion, William Champion, Ware Champion, Joseph R. Claytor, Christopher C. Claytor,* William Cole, Joseph Carmean, George Conrad, George Daniels, William H. Dills, Inley Seth Dixon, Floyd Downs, Abram Fuhner, Benjamin Franklin, Nathaniel G. Franklin, William Mc H. Gillespey,* Wm. H. Garretson, Steele L. Henderson, Samuel B. Henderson,* James A. Hume, George E. Haines, Charles Haines, Enos Huffer, Jacob Ireland, Christian Lehman,* Isaac Lehman,* John Linton,* Marquis D. Mason, William F. Maltbie,* Henry Miller, Robert A. Miller, George Miller, Isaac McGrady, Jesse Miller,* Washington Martin,* Wm. L. Mechling,* George W. May, Jacob Markel,* John Mullenour, Joseph Mullenour, William J. Morris, Charles McBride, Matthew McMullin, Amos Nihiser, Joseph S. Peltier, John W. Peltier, Hiram Robbins, Ferdinand C. Richards, Martin V. Richards, William Rankins, Jerome T. Straley, Thomas Shaw,* Cornelius Shoff*, William Sherman, Jacob Stevenson, William Snyder, James Sherry, sen., James Sherry, jun., Albert Sherry, Daniel J. Shuler, Charles Sherman, Jas. Swisher,* Sampson Sawmiller, Levi Spangler, Peter Tracy,* Milton Titus, George R. Truesdale, Jacob Tester, Jesse Tarman,

*Veterans.

Lawrence Verbryke, John Wollet, Noah Wollet, Wm. H. Woley,* Franklin Wright.

Recruits.—Francis M. Armour, Joseph W. Brown, Daniel H. Bush, William T. Caskey, Goodson McClayton, Horace A. Edmonds, Enoch Greer, William H. Greer, Arthur Hall, John Lutz, Hugh McKinstry, John Motter, Price Nun, Fidillis Ott, Benjamin Pippin, William H. Pierson, Charles Ross, James W. Swain, Sampson Swain, Harvey Shults, Samuel Claytor, Edward Carmean, Thomas A. Maltbie, Anderson Poling, Stephen A. Swisher, Byrant Sweeney.

CASUALTIES.

Promotions.—Lieutenant JAMES W. TITUS to Captain, April 7, '62, to Lieutenant-Colonel, Aug. 21, '64. Sergeant James H. Corns to First Lieutenant, April 7, '62, to Captain, Oct. 3, '62, and assigned to Co. D; transferred to Invalid Corps, '63; severely wounded at Battle of Corinth, Oct. 3, '62; Sergeant Geo. W. Dixon to First Lieut., June 3, '63; Sergeant Geo. W. Miller to First Lieutenant, April 12, '63. Corporal Gideon Ditto promoted to First Sergeant. Wounded Oct. 4, '62, at Corinth; May 14, '64, at Lay's Ferry, Ga.; and July 22, '64, at Atlanta; Corporal Jerome Raymond promoted to 5th Sergeant; Corporal Sumner F. Mason, promoted to 2nd Sergeant; to 2d Lieutenant, May 24, '65; to 1st Lieutenant, July 10, '65; Corporal Francis M. Hartshorn promoted to 3d Sergeant; Private William Mc H. Gillespey to Corporal for services in action, July 22, '64, before Atlanta, Ga.; to Sergeant, Dec. 27, '64; Christian Lehman to Sergeant, April 30, '65; Private Charles Haines promoted to Corporal for services in action at Corinth, Oct. 3 and 4, '62; Private James Swisher to Corporal for meritorious services in action, July 22, '64, before Atlanta, Ga.; wounded Aug. 7, '64, before Atlanta, Ga.; leg amputated.

Killed in Action.—Captain MARTIN ARMSTONG, April 6, '62, battle of Shiloh; Sergeant John Johnson, Oct. 3, '62, battle of Corinth; Private John W. Armour, Oct. 4, '62, battle of Corinth; G. H. Adgate, Oct. 3, '62, battle of Corinth; Thomas D. Crosley, May 9, '64, skirmish at Resaca, Ga.; Abram Fulmer, Oct. 3, '62, battle of Corinth; William Rankins, Oct. 3, '62, battle of Corinth.

---

*Veteran.

Died from Wounds or Disease.—Gabriel Coffman, disease, July 10, '62, Cincinnati, Ohio; Eli Champion, disease, Sept. 13, '63, Pocahontas, Tenn.; George Daniels, disease, May 7, '62, Cinninnati, Ohio; Floyd Downs, wound, Jan. 14, '63, St. Louis, Mo.; Nathaniel G. Franklin, disease, May 14, '62, Cincinnati; Samuel B. Henderson, disease, Nov. 7, '61, Franklin, Mo.; Joseph Mullenour, disease, June 24, '62, Paducah, Ky.; Charles McBride, disease, Dec. 18, '63, Jefferson Barracks, Mo.; Amos Nihiser, disease, Nov. 19, '62, Corinth, Miss.; Hiram Robbins, wound, April 9, '63, Mound City, Illinois; William Sherman, disease, Dec. 20, '61, Herman, Mo.; William Snyder, disease, June 21, '62, Lima, Ohio; James Sherry, Jun., disease, Aug. 5, '62, Corinth, Miss.; Levi Spangler, disease, Nov. 7, '61, Franklin, Mo.; Lawrence Verbryke, disease, May 24, '62, Monterey, Tenn.; Joseph W. Brown, disease, Nov. 26, '63, Corinth, Miss.; Hugh McKinstry, disease, Aug. 1, '63, Corinth, Miss.; Price Nun, disease, May 25, '63, Corinth Miss.; Fidillis Ott, disease, March 12, '63, Corinth, Miss.; Sampson Swain, disease, Aug. 3, '64, Marietta, Ga.; Stephen A. Swisher, disease, April, '64, Nashville, Tenn.

Discharged for Disability.—Corporal John B. Jacobs, Sept. 8, '62; Corporal John Askins, Aug. 15, '62; Corporal Wm. D. Cunningham, Feb. 5, '63; Jasper Buckmaster, July 1, '62; William Champion, Aug. 13, '62; Ware Champion, Aug. 13, '62; Joseph R. Claytor, Oct. 3, '62; George Conrad, July 30, '62; William H. Dills, Jan. 1, '63; James A. Hume, June 28, 62; Enos Huffer, July 9, '62; George Miller, Sept. 12, 62; Isaac McGrady, Feb. 15, '64; John Mullenour, March 3, '63; William J. Morris, Sept. 16, '62; Martin V. Richards, Nov. 4, '62; Jacob Stevenson, Nov. 30, '62; James Sherry, Sen., July 19, '62; Albert Sherry, Aug. 30, '62; George K. Truesdale, Dec. 17, '62; Francis M. Armour, Sept. 19, '63.

Transferred.—Captain JAMES H. CORNS, to Co. D, 81st Ohio, May, '63; Sergeant Rufus K. Darling to Co. A, 81st Ohio; Oct. 1, '62; William Cole, to Invalid Corps, Dec. 15, '63; Arthur Hall, to Invalid Corps, Jan. 15, '64.

Resigned.—Second Lieutenant W. T. WILCOX, April, '62.

ORIGINAL MEMBERS OF COMPANY C, 81ST OHIO INFANTRY VOLUNTEERS, ORGANIZED AT GREENFIELD, OHIO, AUGUST 30, 1861, BY CAPT. R. N. ADAMS.

Captain R. N. ADAMS, First Lieutenant W. H. CHAMBERLIN, Second Lieutenant OLIVER P. IRION.

Sergeants.—First Sergeant W. A. Johnson; Charles Depoy, William W. Merrill, Henry N. Depoy, Lyle G. Adair.

Corporals.—William H. Scroggs, John A. Wilson, Edwin W. Brown, Douglas W. Binns, James Abbot, William H. Logan, William F. Dwyer, John Q. Adams.

Musicians.—William B. Haynes, David W. Buck.

Privates.—William McM. Adams, Thomas J. Beatty,* Joseph H. Bennett,* John Blake,* James H. Boggs, George W. Brinley, William M. Buck,* Noble B. Caldwell,* Charles Clark, George Claypool, James W. Cowman,* John M. Cowman,* Nathan W. Crooks, Andrew M. Dick, James E. J. Dill,* Edward S. Donaldson, Peter W. Duffield, Samuel Edgington, Isaac H. Eshelman, Benjamin Estle, William H. Estle, Elijah Furry, Henry Furry,* William Furry,* Robert H. Griner, Henry G. Hamilton, Edward Hendry,* John M. Henness,* Albert Kinnamon,* Samuel A. Leaverton,* Robert W. Luttrell,* David Y. Lyttle,* John Mader,* John C. McAlpin,* James McAlster,* James McCann,* Calvin P. McClelland, James McClelland, Edward P. McCormick, Daniel J. Melson,* John H. Meredith, Randolph F. Milbourne, Samuel J. Moomau, Cary L. Nelson, Joseph K. Nelson, James M. Nixon, Abraham D. Park, Thomas P. Potts, Isaac Rife, Benjamin Rigdon,* James C. Rigdon, Presley Robey, Charles M. Robins,* Charles Robinson, Alexander R. Rodgers, William B. Rush,* Francis A. Sayre,* William H. Sayre, John G. Scroggs, Hugh S. Strain, Galia Streets, Amos Swartz, John E. Taylor, James A. Watts, Thomas N. Watts, John M. Wiley,* Samuel T Wiley,* John H. Willis, Tilghman R. Willis,* Joseph M. Wilson, Charles Wright, James D. Young.

Recruits of 1862.—Lewis R. Barr, Wilbur F. Cherry, George W. Coaplantz, Frank L. Dunlap, Joseph P. Eshelman, John M. Estle, Fletcher B. Haynes, William B. Henness, David C. Johnson, Jabez Johnson, Andrew N. Mackerley, Arden P. Middleton, John H. Middleton, James H. Pricer, Berry Smith, Joseph P. Taylor. Under-cook—Joseph Gant.

---

* Veterans.

CASUALTIES.

Promotions.—Captain R. N. ADAMS to Lieutenant-Colonel May 7, '62; to Colonel Aug. 12, '64; to Brevet Brigadier-General to date from March 13, '65.

First Lieutenant W. H CHAMBERLIN to Captain. May 7, 1862; to Major, Aug. 12, 1864.

Second Lieutenant O. P. IRION to First Lieutenant, May 7, 1862; to Captain, 1864.

First Sergeant W. A. Johnson to Second Lieutenant, May 7, '62; to First Lieutenant, June 27, '64; to Captain, Apr. 25, '65.

Private William B. Rush to Corporal, May 5, '62; to Sergeant, Feb. 1, '64; to First Sergeant, May 1, '64; to Sergeant Major, Aug. 19, '64; to First Lieutenant, March 26, '65; appointed Adjutant March 28, '65.

Corporal W. H. Scroggs to First Sergeant, Jan. 1, 63.

Corporal John A. Wilson to Sergeant, May 1, 1864; color bearer.

Corporal W. H. Logan to Sergeant, Feb. 5, '62.

Private John M. Henness to Corporal for good conduct in action, battle of Corinth, Oct. 20, '62; to Sergeant, Sept. 1, '64; to First Sergeant, Nov. 1, '64; to Second Lieutenant, May, '65; not mustered.

Private John Mader to Corporal, May 5, '62; to Sergeant, Oct. 29, '62; to First Sergeant, Jan. 1, '64.

Private James McCann to Corporal, Feb. 5, '62; to Sergeant, Jan. 7, '63.

Private Samuel T. Wiley to Corporal, Feb. 1, '64; to Sergeant, April 28, '65.

Private James McAlster to Corporal, May 22, '64; to Sergeant, Sept. 1, '64.

Private Andrew N. Mackerley to Corporal, March 26, 1864; to Sergeant, July 1, 1865.

Privates Charles Wright and James C. Rigdon to Corporals, Oct. 20, '62, for bravery and good conduct at the battle of Corinth.

Killed in Battle.—William McM. Adams, battle of Shiloh, Apr. 7, '62; Amos Swartz, battle of Corinth, Oct. 3, '62; John M. Wiley, Lay's Ferry, Oostenaula river, Georgia, May 14, '64; Wilbur F. Cherry, near Atlanta, Ga., July 22, 1864.

Died of Wounds.—John M. Cowman, Sept. 10, 1864, wounded at Lovejoys's Sept. 2, '64; Fletcher B. Haynes, Dec. 18, '64, wounded Dec. 13, '64, near Savannah, Ga.

Died of Disease.—George Claypool, Mar. 26, '62, Pittsburg Landing, Tenn; John H. Willis, Corinth, Miss., Aug. 27, '62; James D. Young, Greenfield, Ohio, June 10, '62; George W. Coaplantz, Pocahontas, Tenn., Aug. 20, '63; Berry Smith, Rome, Ga., Aug. 8, '64; Joseph P. Taylor, Corinth, Miss., Dec. 8, '62; Francis A. Sayre, near Columbia, South Carolina, Feb. 20, '65.

Discharged for Disability.—Sergeant Charles Depoy, Mar. 19, '64; Sergeant John A. Wilson, Sept. 27, '64, wounded at Lay's Ferry, Ga., May 15, '64; Sergeant Henry N. Depoy, Dec. 15, '62; Sergeant W. H. Logan, July 9, '62; Corporal D. W. Binns, July 22, '63; W. B. Haynes, Mar. 3, 1863; D. W. Buck, Dec. 15, '62; J. H. Boggs, Oct. 1, '62; Chas. Clark, Oct. 1, '62; E. S. Donaldson, July 12, '62; B. Estle, Feb. 25, '62; E. Furry, Mar. 8, '63, from wound received at Shiloh, Apr. 7, '62; E. P. McCormick, Aug. 23, '62; J. H. Meredith, Nov. 21, '62; Sam'l J. Mooman, Oct. 9, '62; C. L. Nelson, July 18, '62; W. H. Sayre, Feb. 25, '62; H. S. Strain, Oct., '62; Galia Streets, July 18, '62; J. M. Wilson, July 18, '62; J. H. Middleton, Aug. 30, '63.

Transferred.—Sergeant W. H. Scroggs to 111th United States Colored Troops, Jan. 29, '64, to accept appointment of Captain; Edward Hendry to 1st Missouri Light Artillery, Jan. 1, '64; Sergeant John Mader to 111th United States Colored Troops, June 10, '64, to accept appointment of Quartermaster Sergeant; Corporal J. K. Nelson to 111th United States Colored Troops, Jan. 29, '64, to accept appointment of Second Lieutenant; R. Milbourne to Veteran Reserve Corps, Dec. 15, '63.

(The non-veterans of this company were mustered out in September, 1864, and on the 26th of December, 1864, the veterans and recruits were transferred to companies E and F.)

ORIGINAL MEMBERS OF COMPANY D, 81ST OHIO, ORGANIZED IN AUGUST AND SEPTEMBER, 1861, AT UPPER SANDUSKY, WYANDOT COUNTY, OHIO, BY CAPTAIN P. A. TYLER, (COMPILED FROM MUSTER-OUT ROLL.)

Captain PETER A. TYLER, First Lieutenant FREDERICK AGERTER, Second Lieutenant JOSEPH M. POST.

Sergeants.—First Sergeant, Noah M. Stoker, Charles H. Willard, Willard D. Tyler, Richard J. Earp, Robert M. Reed.

Corporals.—David Agerter, Henry Hardly, Benjamin Stewart, Benjamin Ellis, William Earp, David Hagerman.

Privates.—Jacob Albert, James Anderson, Jas. A. Atkinson, Thomas M. Blake, Joseph P. Berry, John Bushong, Charles Caldwell, Napoleon Crouse, Hugh T. Carlisle, Patrick Downey, Samuel Down, Henry Down, William Davis, George Devine, David Dysinger, John Finan, Caleb J. Fogle, Jeremiah C. Groff, John W. Gillin, James B. Graham, Stephen Healy, Ephraim Hay, William Helsel, H. Hawkins, James R. Hagerman, William R. Heffelfinger, George K. Hagerman, Anson Jones, Michael W. Kimmel, Charles S. Keys, Levi Keller, Patrick Kelly, Franklin Kating, Jerome Kennedy, Jacob Lime, Elijah C. Longabaugh, Joseph H. Long, Martin Lipp, Patrick Mulhauer, Jared L. Mills, Henry Miller, Jacob Miller, William Mankin, Jonah Mankin, James M. Nelson, Morris Prendergast, Wilson Quaintance, James E. Reed, William A. Reed, John F. Reidling, O. H. P. Reed, John F. Rose, John P. Ross, Elias Stevens, Joseph Stall, William Stamford, Lawrence Smith, Henry Stomb, James Surplus, Anderson Sullivan, William F. Savage, John Thompson, Asa H. Tyler, John A. Vanorsdall, Robert Whinnery, John Wilson.

Recruits.—Obadiah Fair, Samuel Gilbert, Freeman Hoaks, Lewis Lemay, Jacob M. Longworth, John Moorman, Charles M. Peterson, Leroy Russell, Edward Slade, Thomas Cooper, Thomas Shewman, Clinton Shewman, Milton Hapner, Benjamin F. Saylor, F. C. Andrews, Isaac J. Clair, Charles Campbell, James Overholser, John R. Peters, Charles M. Shaw, Reeder Shewman, Henry M. Studebaker, Thomas Shelley, Andrew Thompson, William R. Lee, Nicholas Cunningham, (under-cook.)

CASUALTIES.

Promotions.—First Sergeant, Noah M. Stoker to Second Lieutenant, April 7, '62; to First Lieutenant, Dec. 31, '62; to Captain, Jan. 10, '64; Sergeant Willard D. Tyler to Second Lieutenant, Dec. 31, '62; to First Lieutenant, Jan. 10, '64; Private J. C. Groff to Quartermaster, 110th Regiment United States Colored Troops, Jan. 5, '64.

Killed in Action.—Second Lieutenant JOSEPH M. POST, battle of Shiloh, April 7, '62; James Anderson, May 29, '64, Dallas, Ga.; Morris Prendergast, battle of Atlanta, July 22, '64; Lawrence Smith, Cheraw, S. C., March 6, '65.

Died of Wounds.—Corporal Henry Hardly, Corinth, Miss., Oct. 3, '62; Thomas Cooper, Atlanta, Ga., July 24, '64; Patrick Kelly, Atlanta, Ga., July 22, '64; Oliver H. P. Reed, Paducah, Ky., May 4, '62; wounded at Shiloh; John F. Rose, Corinth, Miss., Oct. 3, '62.

Died of Disease.—Corporal David Agerter, Corinth, Miss., Nov. 23, '62; Corporal Benjamin Stewart, Hamburg, Tenn., (drowned) Jan. 26, '63; Thomas M. Blake, St. Louis, Mo., May 17, '62; Patrick Downey, Corinth, Miss., Dec. 23, '62; David Hagerman, Pittsburg Landing, Tenn., May 9, '62; Levi Keller, May 18, '62; Wilson Quaintance, Corinth, Miss., June 14, '62; John P. Ross, Corinth, Miss., July 28, '62; Anderson Sullivan, Monterey, Tenn., June 1, '62; Thomas Shewman, Big Shanty, Ga., June 26, '64.

Missing.—Franklin Kating, in action at Corinth, Miss., Oct. 3, '62.

Discharged for Disability.—Sergeant Richard J. Earp, July 31, '62; Corporal Benjamin Ellis, Jan., '63; Joseph P. Berry, Dec. 1, '61; John Bushong, Jan. 22, '63; Hugh T. Carlisle, April 22, '63; William T. Caskey, April 28, '63; David Dysinger, Aug. 31, '62; John W. Gillin, March 9, '63; Anson Jones, Aug. 24, '62; Jerome Kennedy, Nov. '61; Jacob Lime, Jan. 5, '63; Jared F. Mills, Aug. 16, '62; William Mankin, Jan., '62; Jonah Mankin, June, '62; William A. Reed, no date; Elias Stevens, Jan. 6, '62; William Stanford, June 12, '65; Charles M. Shaw, May 11, '65; Henry Stomb, Jan. 7, '63.

Transferred.—Geo. K. Hagerman, to Non-commissioned Staff; Nov. 1, '64; James M. Nelson to Veteran Reserve Corps, April 30, '64.

Mustered out.—Capt. N. STOKER, on expiration of term of service.

Resigned.—First Lieutenant F. AGERTER, Nov. 24, '62; First Lieutenant W. D. TYLER, Jan. 31, '65.

NOTE.—Upon the reception of the official notice of the muster-out of Companies B and C, an order was issued from Regimental Headquarters, transferring the veterans and recruits of the former Company to Company D, Dec. 26, '64.

EXTRACTS FROM MUSTER-OUT ROLL OF COMPANY E, 81ST OHIO.

NOTE.—Company E, as before stated, was not a minimum company until in August, 1862, when Company H, another partial organization, raised at Lima, O., by Captain CHARLES M. HUGHES, was consolidated with it. Owing to this fact, it was impossible to obtain an accurate list of original members, but the following compilation from the Muster-out Roll will serve the purpose. On the 26th December, 1864, a portion of the veterans and recruits of Company C, not mustered out with their Company, were transferred to this Company, with which they served until the Regiment was mustered out.

Officers of Company E.—Captain GEORGE A. TAYLOR, resigned, Dec. 1, '61; Captain RICHARD Y. LANIUS, appointed Dec. 12, '61; resigned, Feb. 13, '63; Captain CHARLES M. HUGHES, mustered out upon consolidation of Co's H and E, Aug. '62; First Lieutenant JOHN L. HUGHES, promoted to Captain, April 12, '63; Discharged on account of physical disability, March 4, '64; Sergeant Jonathan McCain, promoted to Second Lieutenant—date not given; to First Lieutenant, '63; to Captain, May 18, '64; Second Lieutenant ANTHONY BOWSHER, resigned, Aug. 13, '62; Second Lieutenant THOMAS HARPSTER, mustered out on expiration of term of service, Oct. 22, '64.

Mustered out with the Regiment, July, 13, 1865.—First Sergeant Charles Brennan, appointed Nov. 14, '64; promoted to Second Lieutenant, May, '65; not mustered: Sergeants Philip Hoot, appointed Jan. 1, '64; Jacob Byers, Oct. 5, '64; Joseph H. Taylor, March 1, '65.

EIGHTY-FIRST OHIO INFANTRY VOLS—COMPANY E. 183

Corporals.—Leonard Ward, James D. Ward, John H. Morris.

Privates, (veterans).—Erastus R. Curtis, Joseph Cushmoul, Thomas Everitt, Albert S. Hickerson, Thomas H. Hullinger, Samuel H. Hullinger, Geo. K. Keith, Jamison Mayberry, Thomas Moyers, Charles Straw, John Simon, Leander Slygh, Samuel J. Vinson, Andrew J. Wilson.

Recruits.—Robert N. Harpster, George W. Longnecker, Samuel Strubridge, John Sindall.

Under-Cooks.—Andrew Davis, Henry Pillow.

Killed in Battle.—David M. Bailey, before Atlanta, Ga., Aug. 9, '64; Isaac C. Deam, before Atlanta, Aug. 24, '64; Levi Garret, battle of Atlanta, July 22, '64.

Died.—Joseph Close, June 12, '62; Alexander Fullingham, Danville, Mo., Dec. 12, '61; Charles W. Miller, Rome, Ga., July 27, '64; Isaac McKee, Nashville, Tenn., Feb. 6, '65; Jacob Shewman, Pulaski, Tenn., Dec. 18, '63; Wells H. Ward, Franklin, Mo., Dec. 11, '61; Wesley Walters, Corinth, Miss., Oct. 29, '62.

Discharged prior to July 13, '65, on expiration of term of service.—Sergeants, Pierson S. Hubbard, George McCain, James W. Hullinger; Corporals, Daniel Harpster, Wm. V. Garner; Solomon Miller, Cyrus D. Smutz, Grattan E. Poage, James W. Bailey, William A. Burns, Alonzo Monesmith.

Privates.—Adam Alexander, Alvero Curtis, Robert W. Ellison, George Fear, Andrew Gillespie, William Gaunt, Thomas Hilyard, Robert Hill, Patterson C. Harrison, John Nott, Amos A. Miller, George W. Murray, Samuel Neely, Jacob Rinehart, Thomas Snider, Ambrose Snider, Louis Swearingen, Isaac Strubridge, William Snodgrass, Joseph Wagoner, William Atmur, James H. Barber, James Biddinger, Hugh N. Biddinger, Valentine Bauersack, Jordan S. Craig, Jacob Gensel, Josephus L. Kemp, Martin F. Kintz, Thomas C. Rice, Jacob T. Rice, Reuben White, Frederick C. Bennett, William D. Clear, Jacob B. Cail, Benjamin F. Gardner, Samuel Kneass, David E. Monesmith, Peter S. Miller, Hiram Nease, Thomas A. Nation, John H. Smith, Lemuel Stephenson, Martin Shewman, William H. Turner, Richard C. Truitt, Ed. W. Walker.

Discharged for Disability.—John Brash, Feb. 1, '62; Michael Brown, Jan., '64; Lucius Curtis, July 22, '62; Chauncey Curtis, Nov. 20, '62; John Fullington, July 25, '62; Gilbert Huff, Aug. 23, '62; James M. Potterf, (by General Order, No. 77, War Department,) June 19, '65; Alexander Allison, Sept. 5, '63; Jesse H. Atmur, Aug. 9, '62; James A. Boyd—no date; Homer C. Binkley, Aug. 8, 62; James F. McGinnis, July 27, '63; George H. Roney—no date; William B. Sheehan, Feb. 14, '63.

Transferred.—Charles Shock to Non-commissioned Staff, promoted to Hospital Steward June, 13 '65; John Alder to Company I, 1st Missouri Light Artillery, Sept. 7, '63; John S. Goeble to Company I, 1st Missouri Light Artillery, Sept. 7, '63; John Hitchcock to Company I, 1st Missouri Light Artillery, Sept. 7, '63; David W. Lamme to Non-commissioned Staff, promoted to Hospital Steward, 1862; Milton Titus to Company B, Oct. 22, '62; John L. Orebaugh to Veteran Reserve Corps, Jan. 16, '65.

EXTRACTS FROM THE MUSTER-OUT ROLL OF COMPANY F, 81ST OHIO.

NOTE.—This Company was partially organized in August, 1861, at Cincinnati and Buena Vista, Ohio, by Captain O. J. DODDS and Lieutenant W. C. HENRY. In August, 1862, it was made a minimum company by the consolidation with it of Company G—Captain Kinsell—another partial organization, from Morrow county, Ohio. The names of the members of Company C, transferred to this company in December, 1864, are not inserted here, as they are given with their own company.

Officers.—Captain OZRO J. DODDS appointed Lieutenant-Colonel 2d Alabama Cavalry; last appeared on company rolls of November and December, 1863. First Lieutenant W. C. HENRY, promoted to Captain of company H, Oct. 2, 1862. First Lieutenant CHARLES W. LOCKWOOD assigned to company with recruits of 1862; promoted to Captain, Sept., '64; resigned Jan. 3, '65. Captain R. B. KINSELL mustered out August, 1862, upon consolidation of companies G and F. First Lieutenant E. A. JAMES, resigned June, 1862. Second Lieutenant CALEB J. AYERS, resigned

EIGHTY-FIRST OHIO INFANTRY VOLS—COMPANY F. 185

Oct., 31, '62. Second Lieutenant MAHLON G. BAILEY, resigned August 10, '62. First Sergeant B. R. Howell, promoted to Second Lieutenant Sept. 5, '62; to First Lieutenant, Aug. 15, '64; to Captain, Mar. 27, '65. Sergeant William Pittman promoted to Sergeant-Major May 1, '63; to Second Lieutenant, June 20, '64; to First Lieutenant, Nov. 1, '64; discharged by reason of expiration of term of service, Mar. 27, '65.

Mustered Out with Regiment July 13, 1865.—Sergeant Marion S. Day; Corporals William Bates, John Hayslip, Napoleon S. Bowker, Benjamin F. Hartwell. Privates—veterans—George Allington, Zelas V. Franklin, James Hoffman, James Kennedy, Abram Lewis, William McCandless, John Vastine. Recruits—William Allington, Charles H. Baird, ('65,) Peter Comfort, Thomas Casey, Stephen Corwin, Clay I. Day, Albert W. Griffith, Adam Green, George G. Krug, Jacob E. Minnick, William H. Milam, William W. Merrill, ('65,) Cyrus Mitchell, William Pryor, Andrew M. Rose. Under-cook—Robert Cox.

Killed in Battle.—Sergeant James Corrothers, May 14, '64, Lay's Ferry, Ga., Corporal Abner McCall, Oct. 3 '62, Corinth, Miss.; David H. Brown, Oct. 3, '62, Corinth, Miss.; Leman P. Gifford, Oct. 3, '62, Corinth, Miss.

Died of Wounds.—Color-Sergeant David W. McCall, Oct. 4, '62, (wounded same day,) Corinth, Miss.; Durbin French, May 16, '64, (wounded same day, at battle of Rome Cross Roads); John D. Truit, July 28, '64, (wounded July 22, before Atlanta); John R. Thompson, Sept. 5, '64, (wounded July 22, before Atlanta.)

Died of Disease.—Sergeant Josiah B. Truit, Rome, Ohio, June 3, '62; Jonathan Burgett, Corinth, Miss., Dec. 11, '62; Judson D Eldridge, Corinth, Miss., May 11, '63; James F. Farlow, Corinth, Miss., Feb. 9 '63; John Hoover, Paducah, Ky., Nov. 21, '63; Abram Hoover, Dallas, Ga., June 5. '64; John W. Joh, Camp Chase, O., Nov. 28, '64; James Kerwin, Atlanta, Ga., 1864; Daniel N. Peterson, Corinth, Miss., Nov. 26, '62; Walter Scott, Chattanooga, Tenn., Sept. 29, 1864; Samuel Stephens, Pocahontas, Tenn., 1863; William Thompson, Lynnville, Tenn., April 5, '64.

Transferred.—First Sergeant William Pittman to Non-commissioned Staff, May 1, '63; Sergeant John R. Chamberlin to Non-commissioned Staff, appointed Sergeant-Major, Mar. 1, '63; Joseph S. Campbell to Non-commissioned Staff, March 25, '65; promoted to Second Lieutenant, May, 1865; not mustered; Richard Laycox to Non-commissioned Staff, as chief musician, May 1, '63; James Maddox to company H, Nov. 15, '62; Joseph Rogers to company H, Nov. 15, '62; Uriah V. Ryan to Veteran Reserve Corps, April 1, '65; Thomas J. Simpson to company H, Nov. 15, '62; William D. Stephens to Non-commissioned Staff, Dec. 13, '64; James H. Tucker, Thomas P. Whalen and Samuel Watts to company H, Nov. 15, '62.

Discharged for Disability.—Joseph Britton, no date; Allen L. Burress, Jan. 25, '65; Abner J. Bird, May 3, '65; John Cnopelinkx, July 11,'62; Jarvis S. Cox, Aug. 12.'62; John R. Dwyre, March 11, 63; Asher B. Ely, Aug. 25, '62; Joseph Gleason, Aug. 25, '62; Marion Hartwell, May 19, '65; William H. H. Kennedy, Oct. 3, '62; Jacob Lofland, July 9, '62; John P. Lyons, Aug. 7, '62; William Lyon, Oct. 21, '62; Alonzo Mootz, Sept. 10, '62; Henry C. Nation, June 19, '65; Silas Peterson, Aug. 18, '62; Joseph Potts, Oct. 10, '62; Charles Ridenour, Oct. 3, '62; Frank Ridenour—no date; William M. Shafer, Aug. 22, '62.

Discharged on Expiration of Term of Service prior to July 13, 1865.—First Sergeants Wesley K. James, Albert B. Baird; Sergeants—Samuel Devoss, Gideon Howe, Ira Hartwell, Daniel W. Potts, Marcus L. Newland, John W. Teverbaugh, William Wehrly; Corporals—James Woodworth, George W. Easter, Leonard Young, James W. Galleher, Price J. Jones, Daniel Cooper, Silas Richey, George A. Crowl, Samuel J. Bunger; Privates—George W. Berry, William A. Brown, Truman Bowker, James P. Brown, Henry Baker, Aaron E. Bunger, Henry A. Bunger, Daniel J. Banta, Oreon Clark, Moses Clark, George W. Cunningham, Thomas Doyal, John A. Ford, William H. Furnier, Elisha Gleason, John Givens, John Gleason, James Groves, James Gumming, Samuel M. Hayward, Robert Inscho, Augustus Jones, John E. Jones, Caleb S. Jeffries, Davis E. James, William Klein, Alexander Mann, Guilford G. Nichols, John W. Porter, James T. Pitts, Wiley Peterson, Samuel J. Rogers, Clark Richards, William H. Stiles, Sylvester Shipman, William Wagoner, Noah Wehrly.

Officers Assigned to Company F.—Captain David S. Van Pelt, May 17, '64; Captain W. A. Johnson, April 25, '65; Lieutenant Thomas J. Harbaugh, 1864; Lieutenant William M. Murphy, Aug. 15, '64.

ORIGINAL MEMBERS OF COMPANY G, 81ST OHIO, ORGANIZED AT LIMA, OHIO, OCTOBER, 1862, BY CAPTAIN GEORGE W. OVERMYER.

Captain GEORGE W. OVERMYER, First Lieutenant CALEB J. SPRAGUE, Second Lieutenant MATHEW A. FERGUSON.

Sergeants.—First Sergeant Thomas J. Harbaugh; Frederick Tester, Samuel Dotson, William H. Richardson, Amos J. Nichols.

Corporals.—John H. Benton, Walter Knapp, William Parrish, David Brandt, Andrew R. Sakemiller, Josiah C. Davy, Edwin D. Randall, Robert S. Marshall.

Musicians.—Leonard L. Spach, Isaiah Westbay.

Teamster.—William V. Beatty.

Privates.—George Arnold, Joseph Boker, Lester A. Babcock, Francis M. Blew, George W. Bunn, Joseph T. Bushong, John F. Bogart, George Barrick, Lewis Bellinger, Anthony Bowsher, John Q. Baker, John W. Boston, Paul Buehler, Samuel D. Bolender, Henry Conkle, Samuel Campbell, Seth Campbell, William Campbell, Samuel D. Clippinger, Isaac Conkle, Thomas Doyle, Samuel R. Detwiler, Peter Edmonds, Beniah Fleming, Lafayette Fruchey, Daniel W. Frazee, David E. Fritz, Elmer Hartshorn, Vinson S. Hance, William H. Kennell, William Kimble, Benjamin Knapp, Robert Kiracofe, William Kindred, Adam Kinsel, Joseph Lilley, David Lininger, Levi Lytle, William H. Lytle, Franklin Light, James Leslie, Abram Laman, John McComb, David McCallister, Philip Munch, Ephraim Morey, Andrew Miller, Benjamin McBride, James Mills, Chas. Nimo, William Osman, Daniel Overholser, John O'Neal, Christopher Overholser, Daniel W. Pence, Michael Philbin, William P. Pritchard, Jeremiah Parker, John Reichelderfer, Stephen Reed, Calvin C. Runyan, Francis J. Roby, Benjamin F. Sherrick, James D. Smith, William Shellenbarger, Daniel Shappell, John G. Shappell, Nelson Shappell, Levi Stebelton, James H. Smith, Jacob J. Sakemiller, William Starner, Louis Stoeklen, John W. Stopher, Daniel F. Stemen, David Salvards, John Stritt, William Thompson, John F. Tunerman, Michael Whisler, Andrew Wagoner, John Ward.

Recruits.—Protector L. Mounts, Milton L. Mounts, Emanuel Barrick, James C. Parker. Under-cook—Sam'l Wright.

Promotions.—First Sergeant Thomas J. Harbaugh to Quartermaster-Sergeant, June 27, '64; to 2d Lieutenant, August 15, '64; to 1st Lieutenant, March 26, 1865; Sergeant S. Dotson to First Sergeant, June 27, '64; to Second Lieutenant, May, '65; not mustered. Corporal John H. Benton to Sergeant, Jan. 31, '63; Corporal Walter Knapp to Sergeant, March 1, '63; Corporal A. R. Sakemiller to Sergeant, July 1, '64; Corporal John Reichelderfer to Sergeant, July 24, '64, for gallantry in action, July 22, '64.

Killed in Action.—Samuel D. Clippinger, Aug. 7, '64, before Atlanta; Philip Munch, Aug. 21, '64, before Atlanta.

Missing.—Daniel W. Frazee, Aug. 26, '64, before Atlanta; supposed to have died in Andersonville prison.

Died of Wounds.—Sergeant Andrew R. Sakemiller, July 24, '64, wounded before Atlanta, July 22, '64; William H. Kennell, May 19, '64; wounded at Lay's Ferry, Ga., May 14, '64; Joseph Lilley, June 4, '65, of injuries received on Railroad, Martinsburg, Va.; Ephraim Morey, June 8, '64; wounded at Dallas, Ga., May 30, '64; James K. Smith, June 18, '64, wounded at Lay's Ferry, Ga., May 14, 1864.

Died of Disease.—Corporal Benjamin McBride, Pocahontas, Tenn., July 2, '63; William Parrish, Corinth, Miss., March 9, '63; Samuel Campbell, Corinth, Miss., March 11, '63; William Campbell, Corinth, Miss., March 15, '63; Peter Edmonds, Morehead City, N. C., Feb. 13, '65; Elmer Hartshorn, Rome, Ga., July 12, '64; Adam Kinsall, Atlanta, Ga., Aug. 10, '64; David Lininger, Memphis, Dec. 22, '63; James Leslie, Nashville, Nov. 2, '64; Andrew Miller, Corinth, Miss., March 3, '63; John O'Neal, Pocahontas, Tenn., Aug. 20, '63; Jeremiah Parker, Lee & Gordon's Mills, Ga., May 10, '64; Daniel F. Stemen, Corinth, Miss.,

Feb. 15, '63; William Shellenbarger, Corinth, Miss., Mar. 15, '63; John Stritt, Corinth, Miss., July 28, '63; William Starner, Rome, Ga., Sept. 23, '64; Isaiah Westbay, Lima, Ohio, March 7, '64.

Discharged for Disability.—Sergeant Amos J. Nichols, Jan. 28, '63; David Brandt, Jan. 14, '63; George W. Bunn, Feb. 9, '65; Paul Buchler, June 9, '65; Seth Campbell, Sept. 19, '63; William F. Pritchard, Feb. 21, '63; Benjamin Knapp, June 5, '65; Nelson Shappell, Jan. 5, '65.

Transferred.—First Sergeant Thomas J. Harbaugh to Non-commissioned Staff, promoted to Quartermaster Sergeant, June 27, '64; Corporal Robert S. Marshall to Veteran Reserve Corps, April 1, '65; Lester A. Babcock to Veteran Reserve Corps—no date; David Salyards to Veteran Reserve Corps—no date.

Discharged.—Captain GEORGE W. OVERMYER, honorably discharged, (physical disability,) Nov. 10, '64; First Lieutenant CALEB J. SPRAGUE, honorably discharged, Special Order, No. 15, War Department, Jan 10, '65; Second Lieutenant M. A. FERGUSON, honorably discharged July 10, '63.

ORIGINAL MEMBERS OF COMPANY H, 81ST OHIO, ORGANIZED IN ADAMS AND SCIOTO COUNTIES, OHIO. AUGUST AND SEPTEMBER, 1862, BY CAPTAIN W. C. HENRY.

Captain W. C. HENRY; First Lieutenant WESLEY B. GUTHRIE; Second Lieutenant ROBERT E. RONEY.

Sergeants.—1st Sergeant William M. Murphy; Harry C. Doddridge, Robert S. Anderson, William G. Bradford, Daniel Wehrley.

Corporals.—John R. Baird, William Bridwell, John B. Young, William E. Walker, John N. Morfin, Harlan P. Maxwell, William A. Worley, William H. Howard.

Musicians.—John Edmiston, David A. Bridwell.

Privates.—Albert Arthurs, George Adkins, Thomas Armstrong, John Boynton, William Burns, Isaac P. Clark, George W. Cook, Silas H. Clark, John L. Cox, Ross Courtney, David Carter, Elisha Decker, Warren J. Dear, Wm. J. Ferguson, William H. H. Finton, Andrew H. Gifford, John C. Horner, Christopher Hockaden, Valentine H. Hafer, Thomas Hutchinson, Alfred W. Hastings, Jacob C.

Hurlen, William Jones, Xanthus M. Kennedy, William J. Kindall, William King (1st,) Stephen Kirkendall, Wm. King (2d,) George W. Kirkpatrick, Moses Likens, Allen Lewis, Benjamin Manley, Samuel Morrison, Ezekiel Monk, James Moore, David A. Murphy, William Monk, Jesse Monk, Sampson Milliron, George W. Milliron, John McGinn, James K. Manley, Christopher Oppy, William F. Oppy, James Peyton, Rufus F. Panley, John Riley, Nathaniel Riley, Peter Riley, George Riley, William Riley, Robert M. Rogers, Philip Smiley, John Smiley, Alpheus Smith, Francis A. Swearingen, James H. Sloan, John Southard, Isaac O. Thompson, Joseph R. Thompson; Miles P. Thompson, Christopher J. Thompson, William Thompson, Isaac Thomason, William Tucker, Francis M. Tumbleson, Charles Tumbleson, Xanthus W. Tracy, Franklin Tracy, George Vastine, William Walk.

Recruits.—John Price, Aaron Clark; of '65, James McNeil, John O. D. Ryan, Patrick Leary, Christian Oeks, Eric Zackish, —— McDonald.

Transferred from Company F, Nov. 1st, 1862.—Joseph Rogers, James H. Tucker, James Maddox, Samuel T. Watts, Thomas J. Simpson, Thomas P. Whalen.

Promotions.—Captain W. C. HENRY to Major, Nov. 1, '64; Lieutenant W. B. GUTHRIE to Captain, May 18, '64; Lieutenant R. E. RONEY to First Lieutenant, May 18, '64; First Sergeant, William M. Murphy to Sergeant-Major, July 1, 1864; to Second Lieutenant, Aug. 15, '64; to First Lieutenant, —— '65; Sergeant Daniel Wehrley to First Sergeant, ——; to Second Lieutenant, May, 1865, not mustered; Corporal Miles P. Thompson to Sergeant, for meritorious conduct, May 10, '65.

Killed in Action.—James Maddox, July 22, '64; James K. Manley, Aug. 11, '64, before Atlanta.

Died from Wounds—Corporal Wm. H. Howard, May 31, '64, wounded at Rome Cross Roads, May 16, '64; Corporal Samuel T. Watts, May 25, '64, wounded at Rome Cross Roads; Elisha Decker, Aug. 5, '64, wounded before Atlanta, July 22, '64.

Died of Disease.—Thomas Hutchinson, October 9, '62, Camp Lima, Ohio; Isaac P. Clark, Feb. 14, '63, Corinth, Miss.; Francis M. Tumbleson, March 5, '63, Corinth, Miss.;

John McGinn, April 4 '63, Corinth, Miss.; Samuel Morrison, July 3, '63, Corinth, Miss.; Isaac O. Thompson, Aug. 31, '63, Memphis, Tenn.; Wm. T. Oppy, Aug. 6, '63, Jefferson Barracks, Mo.; George Adkins, April 7, '64, Lynnville, Tenn.; Christopher Oppy, Sept. 14, '64, Rome, Ga.

Discharged for Disability.—Ezekiel Monk, Nov. 25, '62 George W. Kirkpatrick, March 6, '63.

Discharged to accept Promotion.—Corporal Harlan P Maxwell, June 5, '63; received appointment in colored Regiment; William King, (2d,) Jan. 1, '64, appointed Chaplain, colored regiment; Sergeant William G. Bradford, Jan. 21, '64, received commission in colored regiment.

Resigned.—Lieutenant ROBERT E. RONEY, Oct., '64.

Captured.—Sergeant Harry C. Doddridge, at Rome Cross Roads, May 16, '64; released April 28, '65, tendered commission of First Lieutenant.

ORIGINAL MEMBERS OF COMPANY I, 81ST OHIO, ORGANIZED AT GREENFIELD, OHIO, BY CAPTAIN GIBSON, IN THE MONTH OF AUGUST, 1862.

Captain JAMES GIBSON, First Lieutenant HUGH K. S. ROBINSON, Second Lieutenant, JAMES C. CRAWFORD.

Sergeants.—First Sergeant Thomas N. Sellers; Charles J. Bell, Hamilton J. Sellers, John N. Hays, John A. Schum.

Corporals.—William G. Moore, Thomas A. Blain, Alexander M. Long, John L. Anderson, William J. Parrett, John R. Porter, John T. Collier, Robert J. McAlpin.

Musicians.—John S. Miller, Archibald S. Middleton.

Teamster.—Mahlon C. Swan.

Privates.—Stephen T. Allen, James C. Anderson, David M. Allemang, John S. Baker, James N. Beatty, George Beeler, Josiah Binns, James M. Binns, Mason R. Blizzard, George A. Buchanan, Jacob Burst, Daniel Campbell, Benjamin Campbell, William Caffee, Lafayette Coffey, Mitchell G. Collier, James A. Collier, William W. Crawford, George Crawford, David Crawford, Jonas Crawford, Lorenzo D. Crute, Elijah G. Davis, George W. Day, James M. Dolohan, Benjamin Eddyburn, Peter Egan, Joseph S. Fernau, James H. Freshour, Thomas N. Ghormley, John W. Griffith, Jesse Harper, James Heavilin, George W. Heslep, John E. A. Himiller, Isaiah Hudnell, Junius Hudnell, Garland

King, Peter J. Kline, George A. Kline, George W. Knedler, John W. Knedler, Alexander F. Leake, James M. Lemon, Henry Long, Alexander Long, Richard Lucas, John W. Mains, William Martin, Jacob McFarland, Joseph McClain, Robert McDill, Edward McGuire, Wm. E. McCreary, Wm. August Meier, Jacob M. Meier, Allison B. Michael, Zachariah W. Michael, Aurelius C. Middleton, Henry T. Musselman, Peter Miles, John S. Myers, Henry C. Nevin, James M. Naylor, Joseph H. Nixon, Marcus T. Parrett, Cornelius C. Platter, George H. Reed, Henry Robinson, Alexander B. Rogers, Joseph Schum, William W. Stoops, Philip Stoops, Andrew Stout, William B. Summersett, Henry R. Templeton, Joseph M. Tudor, William H. Waugh, George W. Wise, William L. Wise, Bernard Witte, Harry H. Workman, Grant S. Wright.

Recruits.—(1864) William R. Barrett, (1865) James Wise, John Krautz, Theodore Lorenthal, John L. Robertson.

Promotions.—Second Lieutenant, JAMES C. CRAWFORD to First Lieutenant, Sept. 13, '64; to Captain, March 26, '65; 1st Serg't T. N. Sellers to 2d Lieutenant, June 27, '64; to 1st Lieut., Mar. 27, '65; Sergt. J. N. Hays to 1st Sergt., June 27, '64; to Quartermaster Sergt., Sept. 1, '64; to 1st Lieut., Mar. 26, '65; appointed Regimental Quartermaster, Apr. 25, '65; Private C. C. Platter to Quartermaster Sergt., March 1, '63; to Second Lieutenant, June 27, '64; to First Lieutenant and Adjutant, Nov. 1, '64; to Captain, March 28, '65; Corporal Alexander M. Long, to Sergeant, Sept. 27, '64; Corporal John T. Collier to Sergeant, Aug. 10, '64; to 1st Sergeant, Sept. 1, '64; to Quartermaster Sergeant, May 24, '65; to Second Lieutenant, May, '65, not mustered; Corporal R. J. McAlpin to Sergeant, Dec. 21, '63; Sergeant John B. Schum to 1st Sergeant, June 16, '65; Private P. J. Kline to Corporal, June 27, '64; to Sergeant, Nov. 1, '64; Private Elijah G. Davis to Corporal, Nov. 1, '64; to Sergeant, June 16, '65; Private J. M. Meier, to Corporal, Sept. 13, '64; to Sergeant, June 27, '65.

Killed in Battle.—Corporal George A. Buchanan, July 22, '64, before Atlanta; David M. Allemang, July 22, '64, before Atlanta; George A. Kline, July 22, '64, before Atlanta; Jacob McFarland, July 22, '64, before Atlanta.

EIGHTY-FIRST OHIO INFANTRY VOLS—COMPANY I.

Died of Wounds.—Mason R. Blizzard, Sept. 2, '64, wounded near Jonesboro', Sept. 1, '64; Benjamin Campbell, Oct. 19; wounded near Atlanta, Aug. 25, '64; Alex. F. Leake, July 23, '64; wounded near Atlanta, July 22, '64.

Died of Disease.—Sergeant A. M. Long, Atlanta, Aug. 9, '64; Corporals William G. Moore, Corinth, Miss., Nov. 27, '62; Thomas A. Blain, Corinth, Miss., March 19, '63; Thomas N. Ghormley, Greenfield, O., March 9, '64; Wm. H. Waugh, Chattanooga, Tenn., Nov. 17, '64.

Privates.—James M. Binns, Allatoona, Ga., July 9, '64; Josiah Binns, Marietta, Ga., July 31, '64; William R. Barrett, Marietta, Ga., July 31, '64; Lafayette Coffey, Stevenson, Ala., March 27, '64; Mitchell G. Collier, Corinth, Miss., Feb. 10, '63; George W. Day, Corinth, Miss.; April 4, '63; Edward McGuire, Corinth, Miss., May 26, '63; Robert McDill, New York City, May 5, '65; George H. Reed, Corinth, Miss., March 19, '63; Henry Robinson, Corinth, Miss., June 6, '63; Alexander B. Rogers, Corinth, Miss., April 18, '63; William W. Stoops, Marietta, Ga., Aug. 18, '64; Archibald B. Middleton, Allatoona, Ga., July 15, '64.

Discharged for Disability.—Corporal W. J. Parrett, May 16, '65; George Beeler, March 7, '63; William W. Crawford, May 16, '65; James M. Dolohan, Jan. 17, '65; James Heavilin, Dec. 1, '64; John W. Knedler, Jan. 1, 64; James M. Lemon, June, '65; Aurelius C. Middleton, May 16, '65; Bernard Witte, June 20, '65; Major Willis, (under-cook,) May 16, '65.

Discharged for Promotion.—T. N. Sellers, commissioned Second Lieutenant, June 27, '64; H. H. Workman, appointed First Lieutenant 111th U. S. Colored Infantry, Jan. 29, '64.

Transferred.—J. N. Hays, Sept. 8, '64, to Non-Commissioned Staff; John T. Collier to Non-Commissioned Staff, June 15, '65; C. C. Platter to Non-Commissioned Staff, March 1, '63.

Resigned.—Capt. JAMES GIBSON, (discharged for disability,) March 27, 1865; First Lieutenant H. K. S. ROBINSON, (discharged for disability; wounded at battle of Atlanta, July 22, '64,) Nov. 11, '64.

EXTRACTS FROM MUSTER-OUT ROLL OF COMPANY K, ORGANIZED AT GALION. O., AUGUST, 1862, BY CAPTAIN B. F. MATTHIAS.

Original Officers.—Captain B. F. MATTHIAS, resigned, Dec. 31, '62; First Lieutenant CHARLES LANE, promoted to Captain, Feb. 20, '63; killed in the battle of Atlanta, July 22, '64; Second Lieutenant HEZEKIAH HOOVER, promoted to First Lieutenant, Feb. 20, '63; killed in the battle of Atlanta, July 22, '64.

Promotions.—First Sergeant John Allaback to Second Lieutenant, Dec. 31, '62; to First Lieutenant, Aug. 18, '64; to Captain, May 25, '65; Sergeant Thomas H. Imes to First Sergeant, —— 1863; to Second Lieutenant, Aug. 19, '64; to First Lieutenant, March 27, '65; Sergeant Jacob Young to First Sergeant, Aug. 19, '64; to Second Lieutenant, May 24, '65.

Enlisted Men mustered out with the Regiment July 13th, 1865.—*Sergeants.*—First Sergeant John H. Coulter; Wm. C. Quigley, Hugo Rehm, Peter Snyder, James Casey.

Corporals.—Joseph J. Smart, John R. Stoller, Andrew W. Kerr, Samuel Brokaw, Montgomery Wise, John Scheider, Jacob Smith, Jacob H. Eby.

Musicians.—Daniel Cherry, Samuel Mobley.

Privates.—Levi Asman, Delevan Brewer, John Betsch, William F. Brokaw, Thomas J. Burwell, John Burkhart, William Burnison, Frederick Betsch, Samuel Coulter, Christian Craner, William B. Dickey, Justus Dye, David L. Elder, John P. Emerson, Louis Flick, George Fry, Noah Finical, Charles S. Garberick, Matthias Ginther, Jacob Hill, Benjamin Hoffstetter, Harrison Harding, Geo. Harmon, Adam Howard, Aubert E. Humiston, Samuel James, James S. Johnson, Joseph Mutchler, Samuel Medley, William Miller, Michael Newhouse, Samuel Pittman, John Quigley, Jonas Ross, David Reece, William Reece, Isaac Shumaker, James Stall, Henry Schneider, Thomas W. Snyder, Jacob B. Snyder, George Steinhelfer, Asa Savage, William Snyder, Jacob H. Sulser, Samuel Spiegle, Francis M. Sunderlin, Jacob Wonas, John Wert.

Recruits of 1865.—Lemuel Brush, William Butcher, Edwin Fullenwider, George Putnam, Isaac Rust, William Roach, John A. Smith, Adam Wisenger.

Killed in Battle.—Benton Karr, John Noblit.

Died.—Archibald C. Karr, Corinth, Miss., Dec. 1, '62;

Martin McClellan, Pocahontas, Tenn., October 12, '63; Samuel G. Bowlby, Corinth, Miss., Feb. 22, '63; Martin Elder, Acworth, Ga., June 9. '64; William Gifford. Pocahontas, Tenn., July 5, '63; John K. Garberick, Memphis, Tenn., July 13, '63; Joseph Hopkins, Corinth, Miss., Feb. 10, '63; James W. Igow, Corinth, Miss., July 21. '63; Shannon Lance, Corinth, Miss., Sept. 6, '63; James Nelson, Mound City, Ill,, Dec. 4, '63; George A. Poish, Marietta, Ga., July 19, '64; John Reed, Marietta, Ga., Aug. 1, '64.

Discharged for Disability.—James N. Russell, Sept. 19, '63; Abraham Shumaker, Oct. 8, '63; Samuel Shaffer, Feb. 4, '65; Martin L. Shall, Feb. 21, '65.

Discharged upon expiration of term of service.—Stephen Hasford, June 12, '65; John Madlam, June 3, '65; Michael Tracht, May 3, 65; Martin L. Teeple, May 31, '65; Eli W. Winters, May 3, '65; Cline J. Wolff, June 21, '65.

Transferred.—Walker W. McClain to Non-Commissioned Staff, September 1, '62.

COMPANY B, ORGANIZED AT CINCINNATI, O., MARCH 24, 1865.

Captain, IRA PFOUTZ, First Lieutenant, DAVID KINSEY, Second Lieutenant, GIDEON HOWE.

Sergeants—James H. Tucker, promoted to Second Lieutenant, May, '65; not mustered; Ira B. Links, Samuel Devoss, Charles Miller, Linden Martz.

Corporals.—Charles N. Harding, William Punches, Charles Bosserd, Samuel Touran, John Sullivan, Samuel S. Nelson.

Musician.—Henry G. Snyder.

Privates.—John Acherman, David Bennett, Ferdinand Berkle, Frederick Berger, Joseph Berger, Joseph Branch, Reed Brush, James Brush, Anton Burr, Daniel Capp, Frank Casey, Henry Clouser, William H. Crawford, Elias Davis, Daniel K. Drake, Bulser Duvirnger; Thomas H. Davenport, Downs Eby, Nathaniel Flanegan, Charles Flater, Levi Ford, Martin Gallagher, Edward Garber, Samuel Galey, Thomas H. Gibson, Robert Hare, Frederick Hill, Reuben Houst, John W. Hicks, David Ibert, Geo. Ihemer, Lot B. Jay, James L. Johnson, Geo. W. Keifaber, William Linn, Elias F. Long, Michael McHugh, John H. McKinney, Frederick Meyer, John Moore, Adam Murphy, Uriah T. Nace, Andrew Nisironger, James K. P. Nicholas, Benjamin M. Page, George Petry, John Polson, Henry Resor, W. H. Reynolds, James Reed, Henry C. H. Rowe, William Ross, Levi Routsing, Patrick Ryan, Jacob Sickner, Jas. A. Smith, William Smith, Albert J. Sprinkle, James E. Sturtsman, Joseph Snow, Jonathan M. Tressler, Geo. Wilson, Augustus Wissinger, Samuel L. Watson.

Died.—Lewis Cook, Newbern, N. C., May 5, '65; Geo. Deitwiler, Kinston, N. C., March 27, '65; Philip Stifler, Louisville, Ky., June 27, '65.

Discharged for Disability.—Edward Good, June 3, '65; Samuel Rowe, June 3; Rufus Williams, July 4, '65.

Promoted.—Second Lieutenant Ira PFOUTZ to Captain, May 24, '65; Second Lieutenant GIDEON HOWE to First Lieutenant, May 25, '65.

COMPANY C, ORGANIZED AT CINCINNATI, OHIO, FEBRUARY 14, '65.

Captain RUFUS K. DARLING; First Lieutenant PRICE J. JONES; Second Lieutenant, SETH DIXON.

Sergeants.—First Sergeant John D. Niswinger, promoted to Second Lieutenant, May, '65; not mustered; James H. Forsyth, Joseph Wiley, Charles H. Withers, John Anderson.

Corporals—Albert A. Ward, William J. Compton, Evan Lewis, William Dornbush, John Whalon, William T. Price, Uriah B. Malott,

Teamster.—James F. Pitts.

Privates.—William Alexander, Patrick Blake, George W. Barns, Andrew J. Bays, Gean Bernard, William Barrett, James Cordell, George D. Cramer, William J. Chapman, Robert H. Edwards, James H. Evans, Thomas Edwards, Jackson D. Forsyth, Michael Fallon, Bennett J. Fenner, William Ford, Barnhart Flack, William Finke, George W. Fritz, John T. Graham, William Glasgow, Charles Harden, Edward D. Hudson, Jeremiah T. Herron, Wm. Hitchens, Wm. B. Jones, Henry J. Kerr, John King, Joseph M. Kremer, Theodore Klingshore, William Lighter, Daniel McDermott, William McAfee, Samuel M. Mitchell,

George Miesel, Alfred Qualls, Joseph Rogers, Sylvanus Ruse, John Randolph, George W. Randalls, Edwin P. Rollins, Moses B. Stout, William H. Sellers, James Shannon, Peter Shannon, Emrich Smith, Thomas Self, Clinton Sullenberger, Homer Sheely, William F. Taylor, William H. Turner, Carey A. Wikoff, Jared Wallace, George Williams, Rudolph Zaspel, John S. Zinkhorn.

Died.---Burr Taylor, Louisville, June 21, '65.

Discharged---In compliance with War Department order, James A. Bassett.

Transferred.---J. H. Bueltel, appointed principal musician; transferred to Non-Commissioned Staff; Samuel A. Baird to Company H; First Lieutenant P. J. JONES to Company H, June 29, '65.

Promoted.---Second Lieutenant SETH DIXON to First Lieutenant.

LIST OF WOUNDED.

Battle of Shiloh, April 6 and 7, 1862.

James H. Corns, company B; William A. Johnson, John Mader, Elijah Furry, David Y. Lyttle and F. A. Sayre, company C; W. D. Tyler, Oliver H. P. Reed, Sam'l Doam and Jacob Miller, company D; Lewis Swearingen, Jacob Gensel, Frank McGinnis and Martin F. Kintz, company E; George Easter, John Dwyer, Charles Willby and Charles Ridenour, company F; John R. Chamberlin, Sergeant-Major. Total, 19.

Battle of Corinth, October 3 and 4, 1862.

See pages 32 and 33. Total, 44.

Battles of Oostenaula and Rome Cross Roads, May 14, 15 and 16, 1864.

Jesse W. Baird, William Adams, Aaron Zircle and R. K. Darling, company A; Gideon Ditto, Washington Martin and D. H. Bush, company B; John C. McAlpin and John A. Wilson, company C; E. C. Longabaugh, company

D; Frank Ridenour, A. B. Baird, M. Bowker, Robert Inscho, Clark Richards, Samuel J. Rogers, Durbin French, and William Furnier, company F; William Kennell and James K. Smith, company G; Samuel T. Watts, William Kindell, John Boynton and William H. Howard, company H; Henry Nevin, G. W. Wise and Thomas N. Sellers, company I; S. Shaffer and Joseph Mutchler, company K; Major Frank Evans. Total, 29.

Battle of Atlanta, July 22, 1864.

Lieutenant H. K. S. ROBINSON, company I; R. W. Vance, Henry Garee, John Miller and Samuel Mottier, company A; Gideon Ditto, J. W. Peltier, M. D. Mason, Thomas A. Maltbie and W. T. Caskey, company B; Calvin P. McClelland, Noble B. Caldwell and John M. Estle, company C; Robert M. Reed, Patrick Kelly, Thomas P. Cooper and D. A. Hagerman, company D; A. Monesmith, Reuben White, L. Stevenson, James M. Potterf and Jacob Cail, company E; Samuel Devoss, Ira Hartwell, Leonard Young, J. R. Thompson, W. A. Stiles, James Woodworth, Jacob E. Minnick and John A. Ford, company F; A. R. Sakemiller, George W. Bunn, Vinson S. Hance and John Arnold, company G; W. J. Ferguson, B. Kennedy, E. Decker, T. J. Simpson and James Peyton, company H; John B. Schum, James H. Freshour, William L. Wise, Junius Hudnell, John W. Griffith and Jacob M. Meier, company I; Samuel Brokaw, A. J. Smart, Samuel Spiegle, Harrison Harding, William Reese, Henry Snyder, Jacob Sulser and Isaac Shumaker, company K. Total, 53.

Miscellaneous.

Before Atlanta, Aug., 1864, Captain W. H. HILL; David B. Buckles and Frederick Conkle, company A; U. B. Rush, company C; S. Strubridge, company E; W. A. Brown, company F; Jonesboro. Aug. 31, Colonel R. N. ADAMS, Lieutenant-Colonel J. W. TITUS; David C. Johnson, company C; William Crawford, company I; North Carolina, 1865, S. T. Wiley and John M. Henness, company C; R. McDill, company I; Noah Finical and Thomas J. Burwell, comany K. Total, 15.

Whole number wounded, 160.

NOTE.—The "miscellaneous" portion of this list is far from complete, but it could not be made fuller. The whole number of wounded amounts to more than one hundred and sixty.

RECAPITULATION.

	F.&S.	Comp. A.	Comp. B.	Comp. C.	Comp. D.	Comp. E.	Comp. F.	Comp. G.	Comp. H.	Comp. I.	Comp. K.	New Comp. B.	New Comp. C.	Totals
Killed in action	.....	.....	7	4	4	3	4	2	2	4	4	.....	.....	34
Died of wounds	.....	.....	2	2	5	0	4	5	3	3	.....	.....	.....	24
Died of disease	1	17	19	7	10	7	12	17	9	18	12	3	1	121
Total deaths	1	17	28	13	19	10	20	24	14	25	16	3	1	180
Discharged for disability	6	14	21	21	19	14	20	6	2	10	4	3	.....	136
Total loss by deaths & discharges	8	31	49	34	38	24	40	32	16	35	20	6	1	326

www.ingramcontent.com/pod-product-compliance
Lightning Source LLC
Chambersburg PA
CBHW020919230426

43666CB00008B/1502